ENCYCLOPEDIA OF MAMMALS

VOLUME 4
Che–Dho

MARSHALL CAVENDISH
NEW YORK • LONDON • TORONTO • SYDNEY

CHEETAHS

RELATIONS

Cheetahs belong to the mammal order Carnivora and the cat family, Felidae. Other cats include:

TIGERS

LEOPARDS

JAGUAR

SNOW LEOPARD

CLOUDED LEOPARD

PUMAS

WILDCATS

Johnny Johnstone/Bruce Coleman Ltd.

BUILT FOR SPEED

THE FASTEST LAND ANIMAL OF ALL, THE CHEETAH EMBODIES SUCH POWER AND YET SUCH GRACE THAT TO SEE IT IN ACTION IS TO WITNESS NATURE AT ITS MOST ENTHRALLING

There is nothing quite like the cheetah. A cat it certainly is, but its body has the slender, leggy form of a greyhound, and it has a superlative running ability to match. In fact, the cheetah differs from the standard feline form in several ways. For instance, for a cat of its size it is remarkably light in build, has a small head, and has rather short canine teeth. It has a long tail and a remarkably uniform spotted coat, and, uniquely among big cats, it can only partially

withdraw its claws. The cheetah makes its living by running down prey on the open plains, where it is a majestic but naturally scarce hunter.

The cheetah is the undisputed champion of sprinters in the animal kingdom; no other creature can surpass it for its bursts of speed. Even the fleet-footed gazelles and antelopes with which it shares its grassland home are no match for the cheetah in a short sprint. And it is not just speed that makes this cat so outstanding a runner; it also has breathtaking

acceleration. People who have witnessed a cheetah launch into a chase talk of a spotted, stationary form turning instantly into a blurred yellow streak. Able to achieve top speed in a few seconds, the cheetah matches a high-performance car for acceleration.

SPECIALIZED FOR SPEED

To achieve such athletic feats, the cheetah has become the ultimate of evolutionary specialists. Its body is devoted to sprinting: Long legs and an extra-ordinarily supple skeleton enable the cheetah to make very long, but rapid strides. At full speed a cheetah can whip its body through a stride of 23 ft (7 m) in less than one-third of a second. A light build and small head minimize the body weight. The claws, which always protrude some, act rather like spikes on running shoes, while ridges on the footpads provide extra tread to make fast swerves easier. The

Steve Bloom/Planet Earth Pictures

Norbert Rosing/Oxford Scientific Films

The cheetah rests between hunting forays to conserve its vital sprinting power (above).

AIR PASSAGES

The cheetah's bursts of sprinting demand a plentiful and efficient oxygen supply to the bloodstream. This sustains the chase and also helps the animal recover as quickly as possible afterward. Compared with other big cats, the cheetah has large nasal passages that permit a greater flow of air to the lungs. The enlargement produces a pronounced bulge in the front of the animal's skull, but it is also accommodated by the reduced size of the cheetah's canine teeth, since the roots of a cat's canines protrude into the nasal cavities. Increased nasal airflow is especially important if a chase is successful, for then the cheetah has to dispatch its prey with a prolonged bite and so cannot immediately pant through the mouth. Despite its adaptations, though, it can still take a cheetah twenty minutes or more to recover fully from its exertions.

long counterbalancing tail also enhances the cat's ability to change direction at high speed.

But such extreme specialization certainly has its drawbacks. It leaves the animal with minimal fat reserves to cope with times of hunger, reduces its ability to climb, and leaves it with much less strength than similar-sized cats with which to wrestle down large prey and face off enemies, as well as a smaller gape and less powerful jaws and teeth with which to kill and consume prey. Moreover, though the cheetah can sprint like the wind, it has, like other cats, limited stamina. If it cannot bring down its quarry within a few hundred yards it has to give up the chase and recover its breath.

ROYAL CHAMPION

The singular speed of the cheetah's dash has long been a source of fascination for people who shared the animal's range. Though there are now very few cheetahs living wild outside sub-Saharan Africa, it was in the species' former homelands in North Africa and Asia that the cat was held in highest regard. Ancient civilizations of Egypt, Assyria, and India tamed cheetahs for hunting antelope and deer, and the same practice continued in many regions up until the species' drastic decline over the last few centuries. The 16th-century Mogul emperor Akbar the Great was said to have kept over 1,000 cheetahs

A cheetah lowers its head and snarls in a characteristic threat posture.

for hunting blackbuck, the beautiful but now rare gazelle native to the Indian grasslands. But to trace the evolution of this remarkable feline, of course, we have to go much further back in time.

The first distinctly cheetahlike cat probably appeared at least four or five million years ago, and the earliest fossil remains so far discovered date to three million years ago. These were of an animal very similar in body plan to the present-day cheetah, only much bigger—about the size of a lion. Later fossils indicate that there was a gradual transition to smaller forms, until the present species arose in recent times. Today some five races of the cheetah are recognized across the species' range, although the differences between them are slight and many authorities do not accord them subspecies status.

Indeed the underlying genetic diversity of the world cheetah population is very low. However, as in other cats, strangely colored or patterned individuals do crop up occasionally, including unspotted ones and albinistic animals with bluish spots. One of the best known variants is the so-called "king cheetah," which has stripes along its back and blotches and bands on the flanks and legs rather than the standard uniform of rounded black spots. ∎

(A)NCESTORS

VULNERABLE GENES

Studies of cheetahs have revealed that their genes are much more uniform than in other cats. There could be two reasons for this. First, it may be that the cheetah has become so highly specialized that any individual varying even slightly from the norm simply would not be able to survive and pass on its genes. Or it may well be that the species has been through one or more genetic "bottlenecks" in the past, when its population fell to a critically low level. Inbreeding in the small population removed most of the original genetic diversity and new diversity has not yet built up in the descendants alive today. Such a bottleneck may have taken place at the end of the last ice age. Lack of genetic diversity between individuals is a drawback because it decreases the adaptability of a species to changing conditions. The genes controlling the cheetah's immune system, for example, are so uniform that the population could potentially be greatly reduced by a virulent chance mutation in a disease.

B/W illustrations Ruth Grewcock

THE CHEETAH'S FAMILY TREE

All the larger members of the cat family are descended from the highly diverse pantherine lineage. Two other feline lineages are represented by living species: the small cats of the Old World, including the wildcat, and the small cats of the New World, including the ocelot.

LION

TIGER

LEOPARD

CLOUDED LEOPARD

OLD WORLD SMALL CATS

AFRICAN WILDCAT

CHEETAH

Acinonyx jubatus

(assy-NO-niks
joo-BAH-tus)

The cheetah is so obviously a cat, and yet so distinct from other cats, that it is in a category of its own. What sets the species apart more than anything else is its physical capacity for fast running—an ability reflected clearly in its lithe, flexible build and its long, equal limbs. Its tail is long, but its head is small and rounded. One of the peculiarities of the cheetah is its doglike inability to retract its claws fully into the paws.

Color illustration Richard Tibbits

SERVAL

PUMA

PANTHERINE
CATS

OCELOT

NEW WORLD
SMALL CATS

ALL CATS

449

ANATOMY:
THE CHEETAH

THE EARS

are broad and sit fairly low on the head. They have black backs.

THE EYES

are well placed on the skull to give excellent binocular vision for judging distances—an essential ability for a high-speed hunter such as the cheetah. The black lines that resemble tear stains are a characteristic of all cheetahs and may be used to communicate mood.

STRIDE

The long, rapid stride of the cheetah is facilitated both by the animal's extremely supple spine and by remarkable freedom of movement in the hips and shoulders.

The cheetah is about the same length as the leopard but stands higher at the shoulder. It is lighter in weight, however, since it relies on speed rather than the ambush in its hunting technique.

RUNNING

Pushing off first with one hind limb and then, as the body is propelled forward, with the other, the cheetah launches itself into the air in full extension. Next, touching down with one forelimb and then, as the body continues forward, with the other, the cheetah pulls itself into a fully flexed posture before the first of the hind limbs touches the ground again to complete the stride sequence. Loose joints and the arching ability of the flexible spine enable the cheetah to push and pull off the surface with its limbs stretched far out, adding greatly to the length of

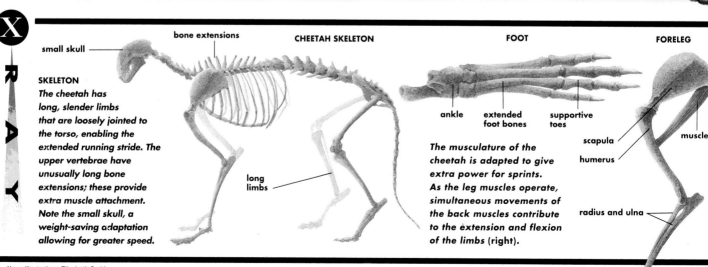

X

R A Y

CHEETAH SKELETON

small skull

bone extensions

SKELETON

The cheetah has long, slender limbs that are loosely jointed to the torso, enabling the extended running stride. The upper vertebrae have unusually long bone extensions; these provide extra muscle attachment. Note the small skull, a weight-saving adaptation allowing for greater speed.

long limbs

FOOT

ankle

extended foot bones

supportive toes

The musculature of the cheetah is adapted to give extra power for sprints. As the leg muscles operate, simultaneous movements of the back muscles contribute to the extension and flexion of the limbs (right).

FORELEG

scapula

humerus

muscle

radius and ulna

X-ray illustrations Elisabeth Smith

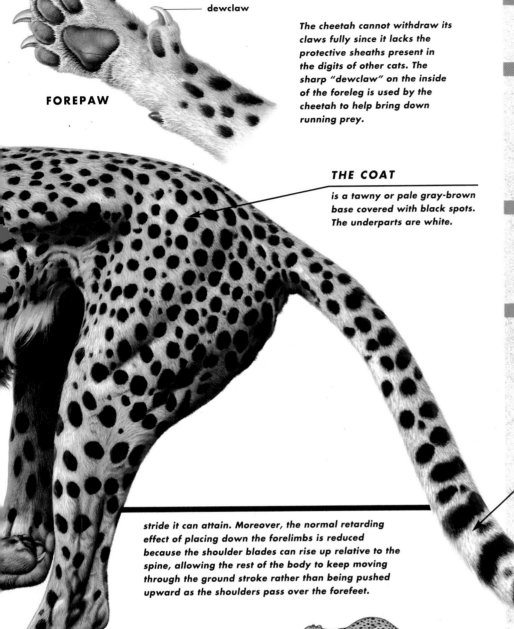

FOREPAW

dewclaw

The cheetah cannot withdraw its claws fully since it lacks the protective sheaths present in the digits of other cats. The sharp "dewclaw" on the inside of the foreleg is used by the cheetah to help bring down running prey.

THE COAT

is a tawny or pale gray-brown base covered with black spots. The underparts are white.

stride it can attain. Moreover, the normal retarding effect of placing down the forelimbs is reduced because the shoulder blades can rise up relative to the spine, allowing the rest of the body to keep moving through the ground stroke rather than being pushed upward as the shoulders pass over the forefeet.

FACT FILE:
THE CHEETAH

CLASSIFICATION

GENUS: *ACINONYX*

SPECIES: *JUBATUS*

SIZE

HEAD–BODY LENGTH: 43–58 IN (110–150 CM)

SHOULDER HEIGHT: 27–35 IN (70–90 CM)

TAIL LENGTH: 23–31 IN (60–80 CM)

WEIGHT: 77–145 LB (35–66 KG)

WEIGHT AT BIRTH: 5–10 OZ (142–284 G)

COLORATION

TAWNY TO BUFF, WITH PALER UNDERPARTS; ROUND BLACK SPOTS ALL OVER WITH BLACK RINGS NEAR END OF TAIL

FEATURES

SLENDER BUILD

SMALL, ROUNDED HEAD

LONG LEGS

LONG TAIL

CLAWS NOT FULLY RETRACTILE

BLACK STRIPES FROM EYE TO MOUTH

THE TAIL

is long, improving steerage during fast chases. The bright white tip helps young cheetahs to keep track of their mother.

SKULL

domed profile

LUMBAR VERTEBRAE

highly flexible joints

The cheetah has a distinctive skull, with the highest point above the eyes, while its canines are relatively small and its cheek teeth narrow. Sprinting requirements of reduced weight and enhanced air intake are at the root of some of these differences.

short muzzle

SKULL

narrow molars

small canines

PLAINS SPRINTER

SPEED IS AT A PREMIUM ON THE OPEN GRASSLANDS WHERE THE CHEETAH DWELLS—NOT JUST FOR HUNTING SWIFT-RUNNING PREY BUT ALSO FOR ESCAPING FROM MORE DANGEROUS NEIGHBORS

The cheetah is a naturally scarce, largely solitary hunter, adapted for chasing prey over grassland and semiarid habitats in Africa and southwest Asia. Seldom active during the night, it carries out most of its hunting by day, relying principally on keen eyesight to detect its prey. Indeed the cheetah is among the most diurnal of all cats, and, although it avoids activity during the midday heat, it tends to hunt until later in the morning and from earlier in the afternoon than the big cats with which it shares its range—the lion and the leopard. Indeed, cheetahs seem to become edgy if they are still feeding or out on the open plains when darkness falls.

While inactive or when resting between chases, the cheetah sits on its haunches or lies down, sometimes in the thin shade of a bush, sometimes on a hummock, rock, or termite mound from which it can survey the surroundings. Having a deep body shape, the cheetah lies on its side. Occasionally it lifts its head on its long neck to scan the surroundings; the cat is extremely hard to spot in such a position, owing to its cryptic coat color and low ears. This low profile helps to hide it from other big carnivores. Though a cheetah can leap onto the low branches of a tree, it is not an adept climber and tends to keep to solid ground. Whatever its choice of lair, the cheetah moves to new sites regularly to avoid detection.

CHEETAHS IN MOTION

When inclined to move, the cheetah walks slowly but purposefully, using as little energy as possible. When walking, it elicits a remarkable amount of curiosity from other animals, even from potential prey, some of which may approach quite close to observe the passing predator. One account of a cheetah crossing a grassy plain tells of the animal being tracked at various times by antelopes, gazelles, jackals, and even a pair of cranes on the wing.

Cheetahs can also travel longer distances by trotting. They do so with a rather upright, springy gait, and with the body supported by one or two limbs at any given time. Other slow-running postures are also seen occasionally, including a low, crouched run and a bobbing motion of the shoulders and hips. Cheetahs have also been known to run easily while looking back over a shoulder and even to bounce along sideways, moving fore- and hindquarters alternately.

But it is fast running, of course, at which the cats really excel, and in which they make no concessions to saving energy. When a cheetah launches into a sprint, muscles and lungs work furiously. Stride length trebles from trotting stride and at least three strides are completed every second. On level ground, the cat seems to shoot across the turf. But uneven ground and a dodging quarry require more changes in direction and slow the cat down a little. The cheetah is quite adept at making abrupt turns, aided by the traction of its ridged toe pads, but a nimble gazelle can often throw its pursuer off balance just enough to make good its escape, and sprinting cheetahs have been known to take tumbles on sloping ground.

After about twenty seconds of high-speed chasing, a cheetah is close to exhaustion and soon winds up the sprint. Having dropped from top speed, the animal can come to a halt in a single stride, bringing the forefeet down together. It then takes the animal several minutes to recover its breath and strength.

THE DRAWBACKS OF SPEED

In more ways than one, the cheetah gives its all for sprinting speed. The animal is so adapted for running that an injured, aging, or sometimes a heavily pregnant individual has severe problems in securing food. A limb broken during a tumble almost certainly

Cheetahs prefer their meat fresh, and a heavy feed usually means a cleanup later on.

Rich Kirchner/NHPA

in SIGHT

SPRINT RECORDS

Though the cheetah is unquestionably the fastest of all land animals, some of the claims made in the past about its top speeds were exaggerated. It is generally accepted now that a cheetah can accelerate in a couple of seconds from a trotting speed of about 13 mph (21 km/h) to a normal chasing speed of around 50 mph (80 km/h), and attain brief bursts if necessary of up to 70 mph (113 km/h). This is still enough to outsprint swift antelopes and gazelles, but the cheetah cannot maintain its dash for as long as they can. If the prey manages to elude its enemy for about twenty seconds, the chase is over. Few cheetahs will sprint hard for more than a quarter of a mile (400 m).

spells death. A lightweight build also means that, despite being a large predator, the cheetah is poorly able to defend its food or its young cubs from other large carnivores—among them packs of hyenas and solitary leopards—and may even be killed itself if for some reason it cannot race away. The cheetah is an ever-wary animal for this reason, and an adult will usually bolt at first sight of an approaching lion. It will even freeze motionless or head off in another direction if it hears the roar of a lion. Occasionally it may stand its ground against a rival carnivore with a display of defiance, lowering its head and baring its teeth—sometimes even trying a quick pounce to land its forepaws squarely on the adversary—before leaping off to a safe distance. ■

HABITATS

Until former times the cheetah lived across a very wide section of the Eurasian-African land mass, taking in a range of tropical and subtropical habitats. It once appeared in open terrain across most of Africa and southwest Asia, reaching as far east as central Asia and India, and shunning only the rain forest blocks of Central and West Africa and the deep interior of the Sahara Desert.

But the animal's range has been shrinking for several centuries at least, and that process has accelerated so much in recent decades that this species is now absent from vast areas and tends to have a fragmented distribution in regions where it does occur. It survives today in varied terrain, including clay deserts, semideserts, shortgrass steppes, parklike savanna, acacia scrubland, and light woodland such as the "miombo" woods that predominate across the middle southern zone of Africa.

The miombo, a characteristic especially of Tanzania, is dominated by the select few trees that have adapted well to a long dry season. The trees grow mainly during the November–May wet season, when some 32–47 in (813–1,193 mm) of rain may fall, but for much of the rest of the year the drought and daytime heat are intense. Local people manage the vegetation by means of controlled fires, and elephants cause significant habitat degradation as they forage, with the result that such ecosystems are highly fragile and can easily be upset.

It has been suggested that the color variant, the king cheetah, may be associated with the more well-wooded types of habitat. Individuals with this

Rocky outcrops and small hills known as "kopjes" pepper the flat East African plains; these are used by the cheetah as lookout posts (above).

KEY FACTS

● The East African equatorial plains are subject to a climatic phenomenon known as the Equatorial Trough. When the sun is directly overhead in September and March, the intense heat forms a low-pressure zone. This in turn causes airstreams to converge, rise, and form rain clouds. The maximum rainfall in such areas occurs in April and October.

● In East Africa, the equatorial regions alone experience two distinct rainy seasons. Toward the south—in southern Tanzania, for example—the December dry season contracts to such an extent that the rainy seasons more or less merge into one.

● In parts of East Africa, temperatures fall so suddenly at night that the emergence of nocturnal creatures, such as rodents, can be timed to within a couple of minutes' accuracy.

DISTRIBUTION

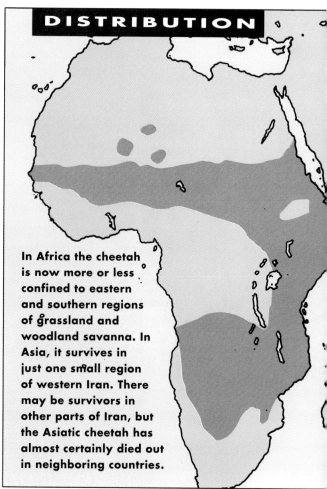

In Africa the cheetah is now more or less confined to eastern and southern regions of grassland and woodland savanna. In Asia, it survives in just one small region of western Iran. There may be survivors in other parts of Iran, but the Asiatic cheetah has almost certainly died out in neighboring countries.

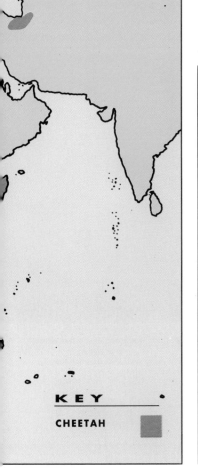

KEY

CHEETAH

overall darker and more strongly patterned coat may be more common in such terrain, where they would be better camouflaged against the dappled vegetation. Most king cheetahs have been reported from miombo habitats in Zimbabwe and Botswana.

A "JUST-SO" HABITAT

Essentially, the cheetah is an animal of fairly dry, open habitats. Humid areas tend to support too dense a growth of vegetation for an animal that lives by running down fleeing prey in a high-speed, horizontal chase. A cheetah would soon starve amid plenty in the rain forests of Central Africa. On the other hand, overly arid areas, such as the deep interior of the Sahara or Namib Deserts, are too extreme in the opposite sense to support the cheetah's needs for food, water, and shelter.

Ideal cheetah habitat appears to be level or gently sloping ground, with light cover in the form of bushy clumps, scattered trees, or medium-length grass. Grass predominates on the African plains, and it is a remarkable form of vegetation. Capable of withstanding fire, trampling, and grazing, it can grow afresh time and time again after its leaves have been damaged, because its growing points are at the base. This helps to explain why the plains can support such large herds of grazing animals.

Trees on the savanna provide the cheetah with shade, and also with "larders" for its kills (below).

The cover greatly helps the cat's hunting success since it enables it to approach close enough to prey, undetected, before rushing in to attack. On wide-open, shortgrass plains, intended victims frequently get too much of a head start to be caught before the cheetah is exhausted. Gazelles can spot predators at a distance of half a mile (800 m). But too much cover in the form of tall grass, thick bush, and uneven, broken ground can present a different kind of problem: all can impede the cheetah. There is a report of a sprinting cheetah rushing over the top of a hillock and then losing balance and skidding on its back as it tried to avoid an obstacle on the other side.

Good cheetah habitat on level plains will also include scattered vantage points from which the animal can scan the surroundings for food as well as keep watch for danger when it has cubs in tow. It is often easy to tell that such sites are favored—among them trees with low branches, stumps, hillocks, rocks, and termite mounds—because of the concentration of excreta deposited on them largely as a social signal to other cheetahs. Patches of dense vegetation are an extra habitat requirement for female cheetahs, since they need good protective cover for their lairs.

PREY AND PREDATORS

But the pattern of distribution of cheetahs is not just governed by the presence of suitable terrain and vegetation. For cheetahs to survive there must be an

adequate supply of favored prey, and, it seems, not too much threat from other carnivores. Depending on the region, cheetahs tend to rely heavily on one or two key species of hoofed mammals for their food, such as springbok and impala in southern Africa and Thomson's gazelles in East Africa. In areas where such animals are scant, cheetahs will be few and far between. Nowhere is this more evident than in Asia, where, for example, the disappearance of cheetahs from India largely followed the decline of blackbuck.

Recent studies have shown that some cheetah populations endure very high rates of cub mortality. Causes of death include exposure, disease, and fire, but cubs are killed mainly by predators, such as lions, hyenas, hunting dogs, and birds of prey. It appears that cheetahs coexist very uneasily with other big carnivores, and in some areas where these occur in high numbers cheetahs simply cannot sustain viable populations. Despite the presence of suitable habitat and plentiful game there, Ngorongoro Crater in Tanzania, for example, has almost no resident cheetahs. But it does have very high numbers of lion, and hyenas.

Altogether, the pressures of habitat and prey requirements, combined with susceptibility to predation, injury, and starvation, all seem to have made

Norbert Rosing/Oxford Scientific Films

FOCUS ON

EAST AFRICAN PLAINS

The grassy plains of East Africa are among the most spectacular of wildlife habitats in the world. Places like Amboseli and the Masai Mara in Kenya, and the Serengeti in Tanzania are renowned for the extraordinary richness of their mammal life. The plains vary considerably in character. Some are well wooded, some are patchworks of shrub, tree, and open ground, some have scattered, drought-resistant acacias and baobabs, others are wide open save for isolated rocky mounds or lines of trees following watercourses. But all provide a habitat for a diversity of hoofed mammals, among them giraffes, zebras, warthogs, buffalo, wildebeests, hartebeests, waterbuck, gazelles, and impala, the adults and young of which provide abundant food for predators. Each herbivore has its own habitat preference, and competition between these animals is reduced because they tend to feed at different levels. While giraffes, for example, browse the tree crowns, leaf-eating antelopes eat from lower branches or from shrubs. Similar differences appear between those animals that eat grass, which can grow tall on some plains. Zebras tend to eat the coarser, older grass tips, wildebeests graze the middle stalks, and gazelles move in to nibble the youngest, lowest shoots.

TEMPERATURE AND RAINFALL

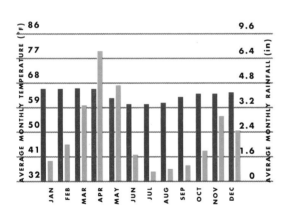

■ **TEMPERATURE**

■ **RAINFALL**

Conditions on these tropical plains are hot in the daytime, but often cool at night. During the dry season, which may last for several months of the year, the grasses wither, precious water holes shrink, and the grass is prone to fire.

the cheetah something of a victim of its own extreme specialization. It appears that, long before human influence on the species precipitated its decline, the cheetah was a rather naturally scarce, low-density animal, living quite close to the edge. Although exceptional concentrations of one cheetah in every two square miles (one in every five square kilometers) are presently found in some national parks, figures of one per forty square miles (one hundred square kilometers) are by no means unusual even in optimum habitat. ■

NEIGHBORS

The African plains are not merely a haven for hoofed grazers; they play host to hunters, scavengers, hares, rodents, lizards, birds, reptiles, and the hordes of termites and ants hidden from view.

TERMITES

Some termite species build large colonial mound nests that provide convenient lookout sites for cheetahs.

OSTRICH

This immense bird cannot fly, but it is a fast runner, and its powerful kick deters most would-be attackers.

Illustrations Joanne Cowne; Secretary bird, lion, and hyena Elisabeth Smith

EAST AFRICA

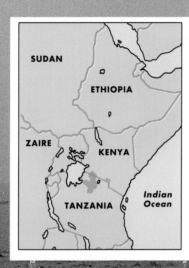

The best known of the broad, flat, grassy areas known as the East African plains lie in southern parts of Kenya and in northern Tanzania. In some cases, such as the Serengeti, the flatness of the terrain has resulted mainly from the ancient deposition and accretion of windblown ash from nearby volcanoes.

■ **EAST AFRICAN NATIONAL PARKS**

ENEMIES

LIONS
Lions frequently harass or even kill adult cheetahs. They are a great threat to cheetah cubs.

SPOTTED HYENAS
Unlike lions, hyenas eat the cheetah cubs they kill. They are deadly when hunting in packs.

MODERATELY DANGEROUS

MODERATELY DANGEROUS

PEL'S FISHING OWL

From low perches around rivers and pools, this owl swoops over the water and seizes fish in its talons.

NILE CROCODILE
This reptile seizes plains grazers when they visit rivers. It pulls them into the water, where they drown.

BLACK MAMBA
The deadly black mamba is a hunter of rodents, birds, and lizards. Its bite is extremely poisonous.

SECRETARY BIRD

Even snakes have enemies, one of which is this bird. Its long legs protect its body while it kicks at its prey.

PYTHON

The rock python may grow over 17 ft (5 m) in length. Its crushing coils can kill small antelopes.

HUNTING

Small to medium-sized hoofed mammals up to 88 lb (40 kg) in weight are the principal target of the cheetah's sprints. In Asia, the species used to feed mainly on gazelles such as blackbuck and goitered gazelle, along with dwarf antelope and the saiga, a goatlike grazer of the steppes. Today, the main prey in its upland refuge in Iran is the urial, a wild sheep. In Africa, the cheetah's mainstays are Thomson's gazelle, Grant's gazelle, springbok, and impala, supplemented with antelopes such as bushbuck, duiker, and dik-dik and the young—mainly—of wildebeest, hartebeest, and zebra. Other recorded prey includes warthogs, jackals, and porcupines, and in both Asia and Africa, hares and ground birds, such as guinea fowl, bustards, and even ostriches, are regularly eaten. Occasionally two or more adult cheetahs may hunt together, but hunting is mainly a solitary business.

CAT TACTICS

Depending on cover available and the manner in which prey behave, this cat hunts in various ways. If cover is good, it may be able to stalk close to its prey before charging from hiding at short range. If not, the cheetah has little choice but to walk or trot openly toward its quarry, hoping to get within striking distance before the prey bolts. Given the cheetah's sprinting prowess, this can be over 330 ft

SWIFTLY SUBDUED

As the victim falls, the cheetah leaps onto it. Using the weight of its forequarters to pin down the struggling animal, the cat then lunges swiftly for the throat (right).

Other big cats use their terrific biting power to rip the guts from their prey. With its comparatively small canines, the cheetah relies instead on clamping the victim's windpipe shut to starve its brain of oxygen (left).

Norbert Rosing/Oxford Scientific Films

GAZELLE WARTHOG IMPALA

Gazelle and warthog Craig Douglas; Impala Ruth Grewcock

NEATLY TACKLED

When it catches up with its quarry, the cheetah employs a deft sideways stroke of the foreleg to unbalance the animal (left). Simply tripping a hind leg is enough to tumble a fleeing gazelle, but a larger victim may require a sharp pull on the rump or flanks with the claws.

(100 m) if the quarry has not already seen the predator. For animals already alerted to the cheetah's presence, 230 ft (70 m) is about the limit for a successful pursuit. But alerted gazelles and antelopes sometimes make the mistake themselves of moving that critical distance closer to a cheetah so that they can keep the predator in view.

Once a cheetah accelerates to full velocity, it is single minded. It selects an individual from a herd—often the animal that has bolted first—and pursues it steadfastly, trying to match any twists and turns until it either catches up with the prey or gives up, exhausted. Pursuing cheetahs have been known to run right past other prey individuals or race through the middle of fleeing herds without deviating from their chosen victim. A

in SIGHT

UNWELCOME GUESTS

The cheetah prefers to catch its own prey and eat it fresh, but other carnivores of the plains are not so choosy. After a kill, a cheetah will often drag the corpse into cover, both to provide shade while the cheetah rests and to avoid easy detection by scavengers. Even so, its success is often spotted by vultures that settle close by. Though these birds are unlikely to bother a feeding cheetah, their presence attracts more troublesome scavengers such as packs of hyenas, leopards, and lions, which often force the cheetah to give up its meal. Given the fact that as many cheetah hunts end in failure as in success, the problem of scavenging is a considerable extra burden for the species.

CLEANLY KILLED

Once it has taken grip, the cheetah shifts its position so that it lies facing the prey's back, safely away from any flailing hooves. The lethal but clean bite takes effect either by crushing the windpipe or severing the spinal cord (below).

cheetah, moreover, will seldom attack a stationary animal. It seems to require its victims to flee first, because it relies on a fairly light touch to bring them down. A trip with the foreleg or a raking pull on the flank with the dewclaw is usually enough to throw a light-bodied, racing antelope off balance, allowing the cheetah to pin the victim down and take a lethal grip on its throat. Smaller prey is usually dispatched with a quick bite through the neck.

Killing larger prey can take several minutes. During this period, the exhausted cheetah breathes entirely through its enlarged nostrils, and it can take many minutes more before it has recovered enough to eat. At last, slicing through the skin and tearing off flesh with its cheek teeth, the cheetah starts eating, usually devouring its prey in one sitting. This cat's teeth are too weak to break bones, and the remains of a meal include a virtually complete skeleton picked clean of flesh. ∎

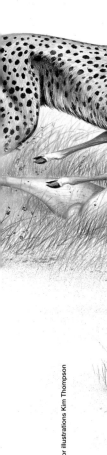

Color illustrations Kim Thompson

SOCIAL STRUCTURE

Like many cats, the cheetah is not a particularly sociable animal. Sparse in distribution and largely territorial in habits, a high proportion of the population live their adult lives alone. When more than one cheetah is sighted together, it is usually a mother with juvenile cubs, or young adults recently separated from their mother. Cooperative groups of males do form fairly frequently, but groups of mature females are far from usual.

The typical adult female dwells in a home range seldom smaller than 20 sq miles (52 sq km). This usually contains patches of cover suitable for raising cubs and a variety of prominent lookout sites, as well as suitable habitat for chasing prey. Cheetahs are notably mobile animals and tend to occupy different parts of their home ranges at a time, hunting and resting in one area for a number of days and then moving on to another quarter. In places like the Serengeti plains, where gazelle populations migrate long distances with the changing seasons, many cheetahs migrate within extended home ranges, sometimes more than 400 sq miles (1,036 sq km) in extent. This enables them to follow their source of food in a yearly cycle that takes them to the farthest quarters of their living space.

Once they are old enough, cheetah offspring follow the movements of their mother, but by the time they are twenty months old, they are obliged to leave the mother's side. Initially, male and female littermates tend to stay together and do not roam too far, but within a few months the female siblings take off alone. Often the trigger for turning solitary is when the first estrus starts.

It is quite usual for daughters to take up residence close to their mother, and in many cases the home ranges of mother and daughters overlap extensively. Females are also tolerant of unrelated female—as well as male—trespassers. They respect one another's favorite sites and time their usage of shared spots so that they avoid each other. If one spots its neighbor, it will usually conceal itself for a while or walk farther away. There is seldom aggression between adult females, and they rarely interact directly.

COMMAND POSTS
Prominent, elevated sites such as rocky outcrops (below) *are key elements of a cheetah's home range.*

Johnathan Scott/Planet Earth Pictures

Females are harassed by male suitors, often much against their will (above).

But there are always exceptions. Whereas the chances of seeing two adult females interacting on the East African plains is roughly once in every 500 cheetah sightings, observations in Namibia showed that about 16 percent of the adult females sighted were in groups of two or more. Since each female was generally accompanied by a litter of cubs, the total cheetah group could number as many as fourteen.

Cheetahs indulge in much production and investigation of scent marks around their home ranges. On the plains, rock outcrops and other prominent sites used as observation posts are well marked with both urine sprays and with dung. Cheetahs spend a good deal of time sniffing for marks at shared sites and carefully depositing their own, showing that such places serve as important sites for passing on social information. Females urine-mark more frequently as they come into estrus, and their messages can attract males from a wide area.

Though scent is the most important form of distance communication, cheetahs have other modes of expression for when they interact directly. The vocal calls of the cheetah are quite varied and distinctive. Moods are communicated by growls, snarls, moans, and a purring sound rather unexpected from a big cat. The cheetah cannot roar, but does utter a loud yelp, audible from up to 1.25 miles (2 km) away. At lower volume this sounds more like a chirrup. It is used in greeting by subadults and adults or to summon wayward cubs. At close range, facial expressions are also important, particularly during encounters of rivalry or courtship.

SAFE HAVENS

Often drenched with familiar scent, observation posts seem to be places where the animals feel secure and where cubs sense they can play freely (left).

Illustrations Robin Budden/Wildlife Art Agency

The social behavior of male cheetahs varies in two important ways. While some males are territorial, others are nomadic; and while some are solitary, others live in cooperative groups. Moreover, social habits can change through an individual's lifetime. Detailed studies in recent years, most of them of the populations inhabiting East Africa, have begun to give us a clearer picture of this complex aspect of cheetah behavior.

Young male cheetahs leave their mother's side at the same time as any female siblings are ousted. But while the maturing females set up home on their own after a few months, males tend to continue a wandering lifestyle that may take them hundreds of miles away from their birth area. Though most eventually endeavor to find places where they can establish a territory, the process is by no means easy, and wandering, intruding males are frequently chased or attacked as they cross the territories of other established males.

Some male cheetahs appear to end up leading a nomadic existence for their entire lives. Others, as they mature and become stronger and more experienced, eventually succeed in carving out a territory for themselves or ousting a previous resident from his. Male territories are typically smaller than those of females, at 12–32 square miles (31–83 square kilometers). Consequently, males seldom travel far to pursue migrating prey herds. But they do compete for the best hunting grounds, and their territories often include a mixture of grassland and woodland, providing a varied supply of prey. Males

also hold their territories exclusively from other males, with no noticeable overlap. Lack of food or water, however, may force a male to leave his territory temporarily.

BACHELOR LIFE

Male siblings are likely to stay together at least during the initial phase of the nomadic period, and sometimes they are joined by other, unrelated young males. In the Serengeti, nearly two-thirds of the males live in groups of two or three, sharing the spoils of their kills. This behavior extends into territoriality, with groups of two to four males sharing and defending the same marked area. Such male coalitions make little sense in terms of competition for females, since they must still dispute among themselves over priority mating rights. Groups are, however, much more successful than lone males in taking over and defending territories. Single males may hold a territory, on average, for just four months, compared with seven and a half months for a pair and nearly two years for a trio of males. Indeed, one study revealed that a trio held on to its territory for about six years.

MOSTLY HOSTILE

Apart from cheek-rubbing in greeting, social relations between males in coalitions are restrained. Individuals are thought to establish a rudimentary hierarchy; cheek-rubbing itself seems to be instigated largely by the dominant male and is rarely practiced by the subordinate of a pair or trio. The

David Keith Jones/Images of Africa

A pair of young males drink at a water hole (left). Male cheetahs seek out the company of others as a survival strategy; a coalition helps them to hold down a territory.

KEEP OUT!

Territorial coalitions of male cheetahs are a fearsome match for those trespassers who fail to flee. Here, a male intruder caught between two residents adopts a submissive posture in a desperate attempt to avoid being attacked (below). Encounters such as these can lead to death.

group members cooperate, however, in marking out their domain with scent—one doing so often stimulating the others to follow suit—and in driving off males that intrude upon the territory.

The typical threat or dominance display of a cheetah involves a stiff-legged posture with the teeth bared and the head slung low, exposing the bold markings on the backs of the ears. This may culminate in an aggressive charge. The normal response is for the intruding cheetah to make itself scarce, but if caught at close quarters it may take up a submissive posture, cringing on its back or one side. It may also look away and utter a moaning cry. In spite of such posturing, lethal fights can break out between cheetah males, either in defense of territories or because of rivalry over a female. Because of such fatalities, there may be twice as many adult females as adult males in any given population.

The black facial tearstain lines are more than mere decoration—they are useful indicators of mood. Conflict between males may sometimes be resolved if the submissive individual purses its lips. This action pinches in and conceals the black lips, which normally stand out because they are edged with pale fur. A dominant or aggressive cheetah will expose the lips, which then form a continuous stark, geometric shape with the facial lines. Because of the cheetah's cryptic coloring—even on the head—the small face can be difficult to distinguish at long range, and it is only when two animals communicate at close quarters that the facial signals can be put effectively into play. ■

Robin Bouttell/Wildlife Art Agency

463

LIFE CYCLE

When ready to mate, a female cheetah makes her intentions very plain. As she nears sexual receptivity, she busily inspects and sniffs all likely scent marks in her home range and leaves her own urine marks as often as once every ten minutes. Eventually, males that overlap with her range, and perhaps some wanderers too, detect the signs and home in, yelping as they approach. Sometimes the female yelps back and walks toward the male, the couple getting down to mating without further ado.

But it is often not as simple as this; there may be some ritual approach then fleeing by the female, sometimes accompanied by heightened aggression in the male. Frequently, a number of males—up to six in some cases—congregate close to the female, and the rivalry leads to much threatening and some fighting. In the end, though, it is usually a dominant, territorial male that has the chance to mate. There have been sightings of a female being mated by several males in succession.

After bouts of copulation over a day or two, the sexes part company. Three months later, and weighted down so much that hunting can be difficult, the female finds a suitable place to give birth. Lairs are often well concealed in dense vegetation, such as within marshes or under bushes among rocks, providing protection as well as shelter for the cubs.

FRAGILE FORMS

Though hidden in the lair (above), *newborn cheetahs often fall victim to other carnivores against which their instinctive hissing and spitting is pitiful defense against large predators.*

EAGER TO LEARN

After several weeks cubs start to follow their mother when she hunts, rushing avidly to join her when she has killed and learning to eat meat (above).

The cub's mane, which looks a bit like a bunch of dried grasses, helps to conceal the tiny creature from its many enemies. It may also be a device to regulate body heat (left).

K. & K. Anamann/Planet Earth Pictures

GROWING UP

The life of a young cheetah

SHAPING UP

At two weeks, cheetah cubs have opened their eyes and have erect ears (above). They also have charming spotted coats and a fluffy gray mantle, the last traces of which are still visible a year later.

SAFEKEEPING

Parasites and odors quickly build up in the lair, forcing cautious mothers to move nests every few days. Each cub is carried carefully to the new home, one at a time (above).

Litter sizes vary considerably, from just one to as many as eight cubs, but larger litters are soon significantly reduced by high cub mortality. The blind, uncoordinated and helpless newborn young are highly vulnerable to predators and other hazards, especially since their mother's high energy needs for lactation may force her to emerge on regular long-distance hunting forays. But even when the youngsters are ready to leave the lair and start following her on hunting trips at about six weeks of age, their inexperience, higher visibility, and poor running skills mean that life for them is still fraught with myriad dangers.

BEREAVED MOTHERS

It is by no means uncommon for a mother cheetah to lose all her cubs to a single predator. A marauding lion, for example, may chase off the parent before crushing each of a litter in turn in its jaws. In situations when this has occurred, females have been known to linger around the lair for several days, regularly checking the site as if for signs of life and sometimes uttering mournful cries. Even though they go out on hunting trips, they may still return to the vicinity of the lair to sleep at night. It is as though the mother cannot accept that her litter has perished.

Not until about three months of age, when they are fully weaned, do cubs acquire the skills that start to tip the survival scales in their favor. Play becomes very important at this stage. In chasing one another and their mother, pretend stalking, pouncing, and wrestling, cubs develop their strength and coordination and start to hone their predatory skills. No longer a distracting liability for their mother, they learn to sit tight while she hunts.

HUNTING SKILLS

At about six months of age, the cubs may be given the chance to practice on live prey. Mother cheetahs bring back live gazelle fawns from time to time, and let the growing cubs chase and paw at the poor creature for a while. But the hunting skills of a cheetah take many months to master; at twelve months a young but well-grown animal may be able to capture a fawn or a hare, but probably still needs its patient mother to administer the killing bite. Many cheetahs are still learning the ropes by the time they are forced into independence in their second year, and since they are lone hunters, the danger of starvation is very real even at this late stage of development. ∎

FROM BIRTH TO DEATH

CHEETAH

BREEDING: NONSEASONAL, BUT BIRTH PEAKS MAY BE ASSOCIATED WITH THE CHANGING SEASONS

GESTATION: 90–95 DAYS

LITTER SIZE: 1–8, AVERAGE 3

WEIGHT AT BIRTH: 6–11 OZ (170–311 G)

EYES OPEN: 4–11 DAYS

CUBS LEAVE LAIR: 6 WEEKS

WEANED: 3 MONTHS

INDEPENDENCE: 13–20 MONTHS

SEXUAL MATURITY: 20–23 MONTHS

LONGEVITY: UP TO 12 YEARS IN THE WILD

Simon Turvey/Wildlife Art Agency

RUNNING INTO TROUBLE

THE CHEETAH MAY BE ONE OF NATURE'S MAJESTIC ATHLETES, BUT THE PACE OF CHANGE TO ITS NATURAL HOMELANDS HAS LEFT IT STRANDED IN A DESPERATE STRUGGLE FOR SURVIVAL

The cheetah's plight in the modern world is partly linked to its natural scarcity: It probably never was an abundant species across its range. In just a few localities, among them Nairobi National Park in Kenya, the animal is common, but elsewhere it occurs at a low density compared with other plains carnivores. This is due in part to the unusually high mortality of cheetah cubs.

Baby cheetahs are vulnerable to disease and parasites as well as to the seasonal hazards of grassland fires or exposure to prolonged rains. Cubs may also starve, either through a local scarcity of prey or pure maternal neglect. But the greatest threat by far is predation, especially from lions, hyenas, and hunting dogs. Studies in the Serengeti indicate that as many as three in four litters perish in the lair, and a further two in five of the survivors die in their first month out in the open. A total of no fewer than 90 percent of cubs die before they are three months old.

Animals with low density populations and limited breeding success are especially vulnerable to the changes and pressures brought by human presence in their homelands. Their decline can be rapid indeed. Today the cheetah's distribution and population is but a shadow of its former self, and the species has already disappeared from vast parts of its range in Asia and North Africa. Where it survives, its situation remains precarious.

Habitat loss and modification is a major problem for cheetah conservation around the animal's principal strongholds in East and southern Africa. The spread of farming continues to modify the savanna on a vast scale; the cheetah's vital ground cover is altered or destroyed, and its natural prey species are ousted by domestic cattle. Its hunting success is reduced, while more of the kills it does manage are likely to be scavenged by other carnivores, and its cubs become yet more vulnerable to predators.

Although cheetahs do not prefer livestock over game, they do prey on unprotected livestock. This obviously brings them into direct conflict with the farmers. In some countries farmers can obtain licenses to shoot marauding cheetahs that live on or wander across their ranchland, but they commonly shoot them regardless of the law. The cats now kill 10 percent of the calves on some ranches, and opposition to them is increasing.

HUNTING AND THE FUR TRADE
Human hunting of the natural prey of cheetah has long contributed to the species' decline across its range. Indeed, this may well have been the principal reason for the cat's catastrophic demise in much of Asia and North Africa. Blackbuck in India and gazelles in Arabia have been hunted for centuries,

For every ten cubs born, nine will die before they have left their mother's protection (right).

Johnathan Scott/Planet Earth Pictures

Cheetah cubs are extremely fragile. These two died from exposure during the rainy season (above).

This map shows the cheetah's former distribution and its range today.

///// **19TH-CENTURY DISTRIBUTION**	▨ **CURRENT DISTRIBUTION**

Once found across Arabia and from the eastern Mediterranean region through Iran and Turkmenistan to India, the cheetah is now virtually extinct in Asia. In Africa, it is now almost totally absent from its former haunts in the north and may well be extinct already in West Africa. It still occurs wild in the savanna zone of East and southern Africa, but its distribution is fragmented and in many cases confined to national parks and preserves. Its main stronghold is in southern Africa, particularly in Namibia.

Daniel J. Cox/Tony Stone Worldwide

David Keith/Images of Africa

Habitat loss, often in the form of human encroachment, denies the cheetah its prey and ground cover (above).

OUT OF ACTION

LAST STOP IRAN

The Asiatic cheetah has been declining for about 400 years. Human expansion, added to excessive hunting of both the animal itself and of its principal prey, eventually pushed the animal to the brink of extinction throughout southwest Asia. The last individuals in Arabia were shot in 1950. In 1952, the cat was declared extinct in India. There are none left in Jordan, Israel, Syria, Tadzhikistan, and Uzbekistan, and they have almost certainly disappeared from Iraq, Turkmenistan, Afghanistan, and Pakistan. This leaves Iran. Fairly regular sightings of cheetahs were made in different parts of Iran in the 1970s, and the most important discovery was a residual pocket of cheetahs in the Khosh-Yeilagh Wildlife Reserve in northwest Iran. The numbers in this remote mountainous refuge were healthy enough then that it is hoped a thriving population still exists there, perhaps numbering in the low hundreds.

Anup Shah/Planet Earth Pictures

so heavily that during this century they have been all but wiped out from most areas, leaving the cheetah hopelessly denied of its prey.

As if this were not enough, cheetahs themselves were also hunted down for sport, even when it became clear that they were on the brink of extinction. The same ruthless attitude toward the cheetah became evident during the 1960s and 1970s when the international trade in spotted cat fur hit its heyday. Many thousands of cheetahs were killed legally and illegally in Africa to service fashion trends in Europe and North America. While acknowledging that

Accustomed to human presence through long exposure to tourists, cheetahs often strike rather undignified poses such as this (above) *in Africa's popular game preserves and national parks.*

excessive poaching was putting their future supplies in jeopardy, traders boasted of their ability to procure as many skins as buyers required. In 1968–1969, over 3,000 cheetah skins were exported into the United States alone. The difficulty of tracing which supplies were from illegally killed animals, and of following this up with legal action, was compounded by the fact that neighboring countries often had different laws over cheetah killing. In the early 1970s, skins poached in Botswana were regularly smuggled into and openly sold in South Africa, where animals were allowed to be culled under license. Tightening up of international legislation has since helped to bring the fur trade under control, but the biggest reprieve for cheetah populations in this respect has been the swing in fashion against wearing spotted cat fur.

Some humans have made the effort to have a close relationship with the cheetah. For hundreds, even thousands, of years, cheetahs have been kept in captivity as sport hunters, pets, and zoo exhibits. The capture of cheetahs to maintain the stock of 1,000 kept by the 16th-century Mogul emperor Akbar probably did relatively little to threaten the region's wild population compared to the numbers taken for their fur. Today, zoos have initiated coordinated breeding programs for the cheetah, and very few cheetahs are taken from the wild. Many zoos play an important conservation role for the species. ∎

CHEETAHS IN DANGER

THIS CHART SHOWS HOW THE INTERNATIONAL UNION FOR THE CONSERVATION OF NATURE (IUCN) CLASSIFIES THE CHEETAH:

CHEETAH (SPECIES AS A WHOLE)	VULNERABLE
ASIATIC SUBSPECIES	ENDANGERED

ENDANGERED MEANS THAT THE ANIMAL IS IN DANGER OF EXTINCTION AND ITS SURVIVAL IS UNLIKELY UNLESS STEPS ARE TAKEN TO SAVE IT. VULNERABLE MEANS THAT THE SPECIES IS LIKELY TO BECOME ENDANGERED IN THE NEAR FUTURE IF THE CAUSAL FACTORS FOR ITS DECLINE CONTINUE TO OPERATE.

INTO THE FUTURE

Across the bulk of its range the cheetah is already more or less confined to protected areas where its habitat remains relatively undisturbed by human activity. In all regions except southern Africa, individuals that still exist outside such areas are sparse and unlikely to survive long. The outlook is better in southern Africa, where there are large populations not just in national parks such as Etosha (Namibia), Kalahari Gemsbok (Botswana and South Africa), and Hwangwe (Zimbabwe), but also across neighboring ranchland. But there are signs that here, too, prospects for the cheetah in the wild are turning sour. Some countries have recently advocated controlled trophy hunting as a means of overcoming hostility toward cheetahs by farmers.

Reserves and parks are critical for the survival of cheetahs in the wild, but even here the animals are by no means secure. The threat of poaching is

PREDICTION

RESERVE MANAGEMENT IS ESSENTIAL

In most regions, the cheetah will survive only in well-maintained protected areas: It is unlikely to hold out elsewhere. Successful conservation will depend on careful management of reserves and improved knowledge of the species' needs.

ever present, as is the danger that cats may wander off limits into conflict with neighboring landowners. Moreover, if a reserve also contains healthy numbers of lions or hyenas—which likewise have nowhere else to go—the cheetah population is likely to suffer from high cub mortality.

Attempts are also being made to set up self-sustaining captive populations. Zoos and wildlife parks around the world have stocked cheetahs for many years and encouraged them to breed, but for this species the process is notoriously difficult. Captive cheetahs are often unwilling to mate, and maternal neglect of cubs is common. Some institutions, such as Whipsnade in the United Kingdom and Pretoria Zoo in South Africa, have been successful, however, and advances have recently been made elsewhere, largely through improved husbandry techniques such as minimizing disturbance during key seasons. ■

LEGALIZED TRADE

The government of Zimbabwe has recently spearheaded moves by some southern African countries to relax international rules over the trade in cheetah skins. They want the cheetah downlisted in CITES (Convention on International Trade in Endangered Species) regulations to allow limited trade in skins from legally culled animals. This is linked to their proposals to permit safari hunting of cheetahs on private land, with paying visitors allowed to take away their trophies. Experience suggests that if farmers can profit from having wild predators on their land they are less likely to eliminate them, giving the animals the chance to survive not just in isolated reserves. Opponents of these moves argue that relaxing the international trade ban on cheetah skins will simply open the door again to widespread poaching elsewhere because it is so difficult to monitor from where skins originate.

REINTRODUCTION

Captive breeding of threatened wildlife holds the promise of using captive-born animals to restock dwindling populations in the wild. Reintroductions of cheetahs into protected areas are being attempted in South Africa and Kazakhstan. Yet they, too, are highly problematic. Reintroduction is technically difficult and is likely to fail quickly unless the original reason for the animal's decline has been corrected. Suddenly reintroducing a batch of animals into an area where they no longer exist can also upset the ecological balance and turn the newcomers into nuisances. Experiences in South Africa showed that released cheetahs could devastate local wild game and quickly turn their attention to surrounding livestock.

Illustration Evi Antoniou

CHIMPANZEES

RELATIONS

The chimpanzee and the pygmy chimpanzee are members of the great ape subfamily, or Ponginae. The other great apes include:

ORANGUTANS

GORILLAS

The great apes in turn belong to a larger group called Pongidae, which also includes:

GIBBONS

Chimpanzees are also closely related to human beings, which are classed as Hominidae.

Eddie Adams/ZEFA-Stockmarket

OUR CLOSEST COUSINS

CHIMPANZEES HAVE LONG BEEN FAVORITES OF ADULTS AND CHILDREN ALIKE. THEIR AMUSING EXPRESSIONS AND UNCANNY SIMILARITY TO HUMANS MAKE THEM IRRESISTIBLY ENTERTAINING

L ovable media stars, chimpanzees have always been regarded as humorous and cuddly creatures. We find instant appeal in their facial expressions and humanlike actions—a hug or a kiss or a wave good-bye—and this is what makes their appearances on television and film so successful.

Chimpanzees are highly intelligent animals that resemble us in many ways. This sets them and the other great apes apart from the other primates, but,

despite their exploitation by humans—and their remarkably cute image—they must still be regarded as truly wild animals that, in the wild at least, lead difficult and often violent lives.

FAMILY DIVISION
There are two species of chimpanzee—the chimpanzee itself (*Pan troglodytes* [trog-lo-DIE-tees]) and the pygmy chimpanzee or bonobo (*Pan paniscus* [pa-NIS-kuss]). Despite the pygmy

CLASSIFICATION

Chimps belong to the primate order. This is divided into suborders, then superfamilies, one of which is the Hominoidea. This is then divided into families. The Pongidae family includes the gibbons as well as the great apes. The great ape subfamily contains four species, including the chimp and the pygmy chimp.

ORDER
Primates
(primates)

SUBORDER
Anthropoidea
(monkeys and apes)

SUPERFAMILY
Hominoidea
(apelike forms)

FAMILY
Pongidae
(apes)

SUBFAMILY
Ponginae
(great apes)

CHIMP GENUS
Pan

SPECIES
troglodytes

PYGMY CHIMP GENUS
Pan

SPECIES
paniscus

chimpanzee's name, the two species are in fact approximately the same size.

Chimpanzees are agile, thick-bodied apes with rounded chests. Like the other great apes, chimps have no tail. They have expressive faces with deep-set eyes, a flat nose, and a wide, protruding mouth. Large, round ears stick out clearly from their head. Their long arms dangle down below their knees when they stand upright, and their slender hands have thickened knuckles that provide support when walking on all fours.

Chimps have long, thin fingers and a humanlike thumb, and these make them extremely skillful with their hands. Their large teeth, with long canines and flat molars, are adapted for chewing fruit.

THE PYGMY CHIMPANZEE HAS BEEN RECOGNIZED AS A SEPARATE SPECIES ONLY SINCE THE 1930s

The pygmy chimpanzee is very similar to the common chimpanzee, and it was not until 1933 that zoologists decided it was a separate species. However, it is somewhat slighter in build than the common chimp, with a smaller head, narrow shoulders, longer limbs, and a more slender body. Its face is always black, with reddish lips, and it has tufts of long, fine hair over its ears.

Michael Dick/Animals Animals/OSF

In spite of its name, the pygmy chimp, or bonobo, (above) *is around the same height as the common* chimp (right), *though it has a somewhat slighter build.*

Tom Brakefield

WHAT IS A PRIMATE?

The primates are an order of mammals containing 183 different species. Their name derives from the Latin *primus,* or "first"—meaning first in order of importance—as some of them are among the most intelligent of all animals.

One of their most important adaptations is the way their hands and feet have evolved for gripping objects: They have "opposable," or grasping, thumbs or toes, as well as more or less flat nails instead of the more primitive claws. Other features include a flattened face, large brain, and forward-facing eyes.

Most primates live in the trees and walk on all fours, though some, such as the gorillas, chimps, and gibbons, are also capable of walking upright.

The first recognizable apes were present deep within the forests of Africa about 20 million years ago. These primitive apes resembled a female gorilla in size, and their teeth were similar to those of modern apes, with large incisors and canines and small molars. Like present-day chimps, they were probably mainly fruit eaters, though, unlike them, they lived mostly in trees and probably moved on the ground on all fours. They had long, monkeylike bodies, apelike limbs, and no tail. It is now believed that these same animals were the ancestors of humans as well.

> THE PREHISTORIC APES WERE MORE LIKE GIANT VERSIONS OF MODERN ORANGUTANS THAN CHIMPANZEES

Around 15 million years ago, the early ape *Sivapithecus* (seev-a-PITH-eh-kuss) appeared. It was a large creature with strong jaws for devouring tough vegetation. Its closest relative, *Gigantopithecus* (jie-gant-o-PITH-eh-kuss), was a huge ape that survived into the Pleistocene, about 2 million years ago, in China. Males may have reached a height of 8 feet (2.5 meters).

In the 19th century, the naturalist Charles Darwin first noticed the similarities between the great apes and ourselves—such as the large brain, the ability to walk on hind legs, the opposable thumb, the structure of the face, the barrel-shaped chest, and maternal care of young—and, from this, he developed his revolutionary theories on the

473

evolution of humans. Since then, his views have been strengthened by discoveries of fossil forms of early man, which were apelike in appearance. One example was *Australopithecus* (o-stral-o-PITH-eh-kuss), which lived in Africa between 4 and 1 million years ago. Its lifestyle was probably somewhere between that of apes and the early forms of *Homo sapiens*, or modern humans.

THE EVOLUTIONARY PATH LINKING APES AND HUMANS MAY SOON BE REVEALED BY NEW SCIENTIFIC METHODS

So far, the known fossil record is not complete enough to give a full picture of the evolution of humans and their relationship to the other great apes. New techniques in molecular genetics are helping to fill in some of the missing pieces of the puzzle.

TOO CLOSE FOR COMFORT?

DNA (deoxyribonucleic acid) is the molecule at the heart of genetic inheritance. Now, by studying the DNA of related species, scientists can find out how closely related two different animals are.

Some scientists now calculate that the evolutionary line leading to the gorilla branched off the line leading to humans and chimpanzees about 8 million years ago. The chimpanzee/human split probably occurred about 4 million years ago, making chimpanzees the closest living relative to humans, sharing over 98 percent of the same DNA. ■

THE DESCENT OF MAN

Charles Darwin caused a public outcry with his theory of evolution, which claimed that, as humans and apes had many characteristics in common—both physical and psychological—it was likely that they shared the same ancestor. Until then, it was generally accepted that humans were created by God, as described in the Book of Genesis.

Darwin, however, said that all creatures, including humans, had evolved as species by a process of natural selection in which only the fittest survived, passing on their successful characteristics to their offspring.

Darwin's theories survived the storm of criticism and, by undermining established scientific thought, paved the way for the development of current evolutionary theory.

THE CHIMPANZEE'S FAMILY TREE

This family tree shows the complex subdivisions of the primate order. This order contains a wide range of species, from the prosimians, or "lower primates"—which include the lemurs, galagos, lorises, and tarsiers—to the more advanced "higher primates"—monkeys, apes, and humans.

In the early years of the 20th century, it was thought there were as many as fourteen varieties of the common chimpanzee; now only three are recognized.

COMMON CHIMPANZEE

Pan troglodytes

(pan trog-lo-DIE-tees)

The chimpanzee is one of the four species of great ape. All of them are large primates with long arms, heavy, barrel-chested bodies, and no obvious tails. Another great ape feature is the large head, which houses a well-developed skull.

There are three varieties, or subspecies, of the common chimpanzee. These are found in different parts of Africa, and their populations do not overlap.

SUBSPECIES:

CENTRAL AFRICAN CHIMPANZEE

EAST AFRICAN CHIMPANZEE

WEST AFRICAN CHIMPANZEE

NEW WORLD MONKEYS

OLD WORLD MONKEYS

Illustrations Peter David Scott

PYGMY CHIMPANZEE

Pan paniscus

(pan pa-NIS-kuss)

The pygmy chimpanzee differs from the common chimp in its build, as well as in its chosen habitat and behavior.

The pygmy chimp has longer limbs than the common species, and a narrower chest. It also has more hair, and, on the head, tufts spread out over the ears to either side. Its face is black. The skeleton and skull are very similar, except that the pygmy chimp has smaller teeth, especially the molars.

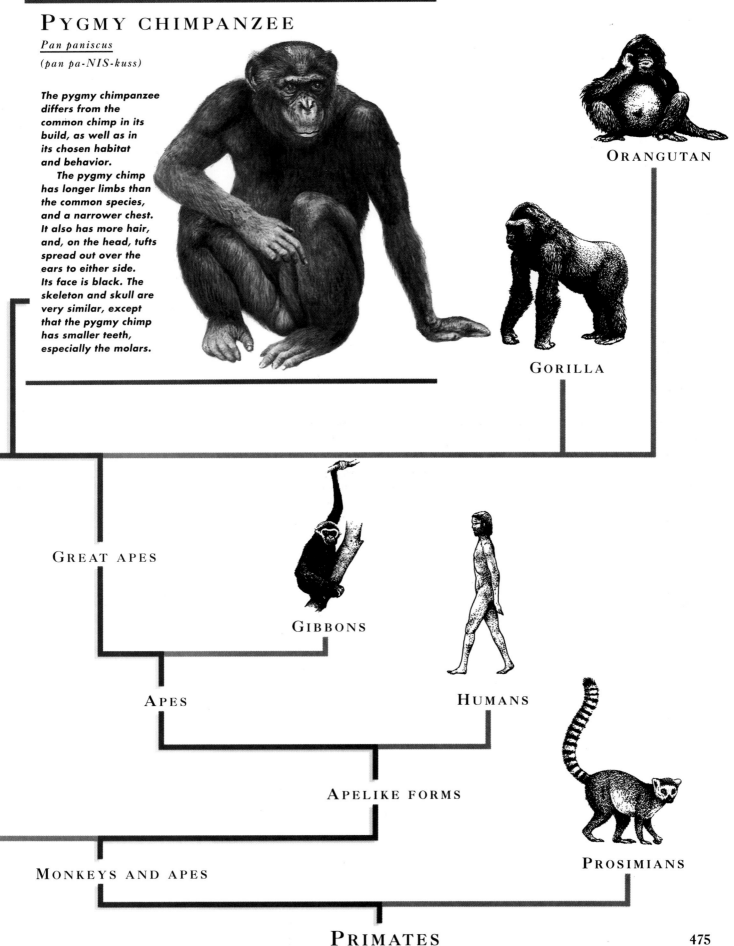

ORANGUTAN

GORILLA

GREAT APES

GIBBONS

HUMANS

APES

APELIKE FORMS

PROSIMIANS

MONKEYS AND APES

PRIMATES

475

ANATOMY: THE CHIMPANZEE

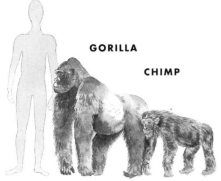

GORILLA

CHIMP

The head-and-body length of a male chimp measures about 30–36 in (76–91 cm), considerably smaller than a gorilla, the largest of the great apes, and smaller than some humans.

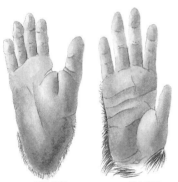

FOOT   HAND

Strong hands and feet provide a firm grip. When the chimp is climbing, the foot's big toe, which can be spread like a thumb, helps to push the animal upward.

The chimp's "opposable" thumb is a feature it shares with humans and other primates. It allows it to handle small objects such as this berry and to use a number of tools.

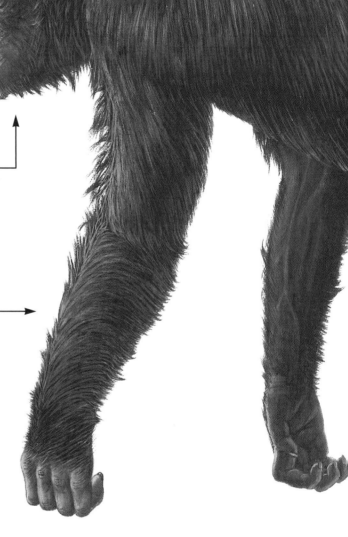

A CHIMP'S FACE

is very expressive, largely because of the animal's protruding muzzle and flexible lips.

THICK, MUSCULAR

arms are more flexible than the legs, and reach to just below knee level when the chimp stands erect.

X SKELETON

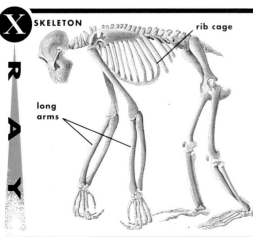

rib cage

long arms

X RAY

This view of a chimpanzee skeleton shows the very long limbs, hands, and feet, in the typical "knuckle-walk" position. In contrast, the trunk is relatively small. The rib cage, though short, is quite large, reflecting the chimp's broad, muscular chest and shoulders.

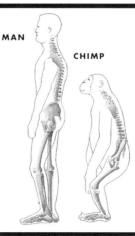

MAN

CHIMP

Although chimpanzees can stand upright for a short time, they can never stand erect in the way that humans do. This is because their spine and their legs are curved, and an upright stance causes too much strain on the spine and leg muscles to be permanent.

X-ray illustrations Elisabeth Smith

The cerebellum, that part of the brain which controls problem-solving activities, is highly developed among chimps. It is exceeded in its complexity only by that of humans.

CHIMPANZEE **MAN**

cerebellum

LIKE HUMANS, chimps are covered in hair, though theirs is thicker and covers their whole body apart from the genital area, palms, and soles.

CLASSIFICATION

GENUS: *PAN*

SPECIES: *TROGLODYTES*

SIZE

BODY LENGTH/MALE: 30–36 IN (76–91 CM)

BODY LENGTH/FEMALE: 28–33 IN (71–84 CM)

WEIGHT/MALE: 88 LB (40 KG)

WEIGHT/FEMALE: 66 LB (30 KG)

WEIGHT AT BIRTH: 2–4 LB (0.9–1.8 KG)

COLORATION

VARIES GEOGRAPHICALLY: MAINLY BLACK, THOUGH AFTER ABOUT 20 YEARS GRAY HAIR ON BACK IS COMMON. SKIN IS BLACK ON HANDS AND FEET. FACE CHANGES WITH AGE FROM PINK TO BROWN TO BLACK. BOTH SEXES OFTEN HAVE A SHORT WHITE BEARD, AND A BALD TRIANGLE ON THE FOREHEAD IS PARTICULARLY COMMON IN FEMALES

FEATURES

LONG, MUSCULAR LIMBS

STRONG, STOUT BODY

LARGE HEADS WITH PROMINENT MUZZLE, A STRONG BROW RIDGE, LARGE PROTRUDING EARS, AND DEEP-SET EYES

GRASPING FEET AND HANDS WITH OPPOSABLE THUMB

FLEXIBLE ANKLE joints, muscular legs, and large feet with slender toes and an extended big toe combine to make the chimpanzee a strong tree-climber.

Main Illustration Barry Croucher/Wildlife Art Agency

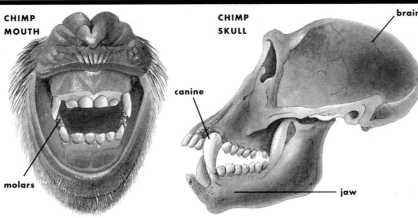

The chimpanzee's prominent mouth can make a considerable noise, though it is not capable of true speech. Its teeth, at least in comparison with those of humans, are rather large, though its molars are smaller than those of a gorilla. This reflects its largely fruit-based diet.

CHIMP MOUTH

molars

CHIMP SKULL

canine

jaw

braincase

The skull of an adult chimpanzee features strong projecting jaws, deep-set eye sockets, and a large cavity for its sizable brain. Note the extended canine teeth, which grow particularly long in adult males and are often used in vicious, sometimes fatal, fights.

FRIENDS AND RELATIONS

THE COMPLEX SOCIAL BEHAVIOR OF THE CHIMPANZEE POINTS TO A CREATURE OF RARE INTELLIGENCE—BUT DOES THE CHIMPANZEE SHARE WITH HUMANS THE ABILITY TO COMMUNICATE THROUGH LANGUAGE?

C himpanzees number among the most intelligent of all animals. They lead complex social lives, communicate with each other using a wide range of facial expressions, signs, and sounds, use tools on a regular basis, and are able to solve a great variety of problems by reason alone. Recent scientific research suggests they may even be able to communicate using a complex symbolic language.

RICH AND VARIED
The behavior of chimpanzees is at its richest and most varied in the wild. From early dawn, when the chimps begin to descend noisily from their trees and scramble down to the forest floor, until late in the evening, when they prepare fresh nests for the night, they live extraordinarily complex lives.

Intrigued by such behavior, many scientists

> THE SOUNDS MADE BY CHIMPS CAN BE DEAFENING—LIKE CHILDREN, THEY SEEM TO RELISH NOISE FOR ITS OWN SAKE

have embarked on long-term studies of the chimp. What interests them in particular is their ability to communicate and to learn new behavior patterns. It is this adaptability that allows chimps to exploit new and differing environments.

Studies have shown that individual chimpanzees can be taught complicated skills, such as using keys to open locks, distinguishing between differently shaped blocks, and identifying photographs.

Measuring animal intelligence has its pitfalls, considering that the concept of intelligence has a tremendously human bias. However, the evidence suggests that chimpanzees possess some of the problem-solving abilities typical of humans. While the diversity of mammals clearly indicates that

intelligence is not the only key to survival, it appears to be a critical factor for humans and their great ape relatives.

A UNIQUE SKILL?
Most people (including scientists), when distinguishing the single most important feature that separates humans from all other animals, would point to the use of a spoken language. It is a skill long thought unique to *Homo sapiens*. For this reason, many studies of chimpanzee behavior have concentrated on trying to teach them to speak.

Tom Brakefield

An adult chimp in a thoughtful mood. The real nature of chimp intelligence is the subject of heated debate.

Peter Davey/Bruce Coleman Ltd.

Tom McHugh/Photo Researchers-ZEFA

Prolonged infant care (left) *and the ability to use tools* (above) *are among the many characteristics chimpanzees share with humans.*

Early attempts failed, owing to fundamental differences in the physical makeup of chimps and humans: The voice box of the chimpanzee seems to be incapable of making a subtle enough range of sounds to allow true speech development. Another difficulty was that the animals being taught were too old and set in their ways. Younger chimps, on the other hand, are more compliant, eager to collaborate with their new

> EMINENT THINKERS HAVE DRAWN ATTENTION TO THE MORAL PROBLEMS PRESENTED BY SCIENTIFIC RESEARCH

scientific family.

Recently, at several universities, there have been breakthrough studies that appear to suggest that, when young, both species of chimpanzee can be taught to use language and are able to talk to their keepers.

However, moral questions abound: If there really is little difference in intelligence between a chimpanzee and, say, a two-year-old child, should such creatures be held in captivity? Should they be the subject of medical experiments? Should their endangered environment be subject to the kind of protection one would expect if it contained helpless human children? This is one moral debate that is certain to be long and controversial. ∎

HABITATS

Steve Robinson/NHPA

Chimpanzees, like this juvenile (left), *are basically arboreal, or tree-living, animals, though they can move across the ground on all fours equally well. Their preferred habitat is rain forest, but they will also live in savanna and grasslands, providing there is some woodland cover.*

Although the ideal habitat for chimpanzees is damp tropical forest, these highly adaptable creatures can also be found in deciduous woodland and in drier areas such as savanna and grassland.

In the past, chimpanzees were found in a broad swath from the Atlantic coast of central Africa almost to the western shore of Lake Victoria. The picture nowadays is one of declining numbers, where chimps persist only in separate pockets—mostly in central Africa, which contains about 80

IN THE IVORY COAST AND LIBERIA, CHIMPANZEES ARE LOSING THEIR FOREST HOMES TO OIL PALM AND RUBBER PLANTATIONS

---

percent of Africa's remaining tropical forest, particularly in Zaire, Gabon, and Cameroon. Pygmy chimpanzees, which have always had a much smaller range than common chimpanzees, favor the dense, rich rain forest of central Zaire.

RICH VARIETY

The climate in the tropical rain forest is constantly warm and wet. The Zaire rain forest, the largest in the whole of Africa, contains thousands of species of plants, the commonest of which belong to the pea and mahogany families. In fact, Zaire has more plant species than any other African country—over 11,000. The vast majority of these are to be found in the country's dense tropical rain forests, and a third of them cannot be found anywhere else in the

world. The forests also contain over 400 species of mammals, including gorillas, okapis, and elephants.

In the western part of the chimpanzee's range, especially in the Ivory Coast and Liberia, the forests have been much more affected by clearance and other disturbances. Large areas have been cut down for timber and used for agriculture. Land that once supported rich rain forest now has plantations of oil palm or rubber—and no place for chimps.

BEYOND THE RAIN FOREST

In the region's few remaining forests, rainfall varies over the year and there is a definite dry season. In the forests of Sierra Leone, for example, the rainfall may be as high as 131 inches (3,400 millimeters) a year, but this includes a dry period of three or four months. Here, the vegetation is known as tropical

FOCUS ON

THE ZAIRE RAIN FOREST

The rain forest of Zaire in central Africa is a constant, stable world of humid warmth, producing an abundance of fruit, insects, and vegetation. Annual rainfall can be as much as 120 inches (3,048 millimeters), spread evenly throughout the year, and the temperature varies between 68 and 86°F (20 and 30°C) during the course of a day. As most of the trees are evergreen, there is a permanent canopy over the forest with clearings only where trees have fallen.

It is ideal habitat for the chimpanzee—there are few predators and the trees provide safety at night when the chimps build their nests high in the branches. The trees also yield much of the food and moisture necessary to the chimp's diet.

Tim Laman/The Wildlife Collection

seasonal forest. If the dry period is longer than this, savanna replaces the forest.

Outside the main zone of the rain forests, both to the north and the south, the rains are too irregular to support closed forest and there is open woodland, savanna, or grassland, depending on the kind of soil and the rainfall pattern. The savanna usually receives only 40 to 59 inches (1,000 to 1,500 millimeters) of rain a year, with a dry season lasting anywhere between four and six months.

In these drier areas, chimpanzees seek out sites with clumps of trees, such as river valleys or gullies. In the driest parts, the trees thin out and gradually disappear, giving way to open, arid grassland. As chimps like to live within reach of good supplies of water, they usually avoid these areas.

In the savanna, chimps share their habitat with

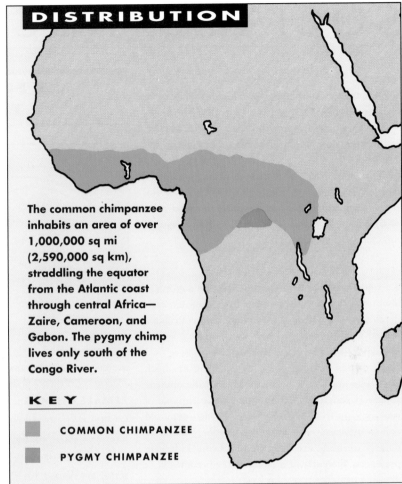

DISTRIBUTION

The common chimpanzee inhabits an area of over 1,000,000 sq mi (2,590,000 sq km), straddling the equator from the Atlantic coast through central Africa—Zaire, Cameroon, and Gabon. The pygmy chimp lives only south of the Congo River.

KEY

■ COMMON CHIMPANZEE

■ PYGMY CHIMPANZEE

THE FOREST LAYERS

EMERGENT TREES
Dwarf galago
100 ft (30 m)
Bosman's potto
CANOPY
Mona monkey
Colobus monkey
50 ft (15 m)
Mangabey
MIDDLE LAYER
25 ft (7.6 m)
Chimpanzee
Gorilla
SHRUB LAYER

The world's richest ecosystem, the African rain forest forms a stable environment where a variety of creatures live and eat at different levels. The top layer consists of scattered tall trees, towering above the next layer, the canopy, where the treetops meet. Next comes the middle layer and then the layer where shrubs grow. Below this there may be a sparse herb layer.

Illustration Kou Kang Chen

large predators such as lions, leopards, and cheetahs, as well as jackals and hyenas, and vultures who feed on carrion. Herbivores include elephants, giraffe, bushbuck, buffalo, and warthogs. There are other primates in the savanna, too—olive and savanna baboons, patas monkeys, and vervet monkeys. ■

KEY FACTS

● It is estimated that there is now a population of up to 200,000 chimps and pygmy chimps in Africa, ranging over 15 countries.

● Chimps thrive in tropical rain forests, but they may also be found in drier conditions and higher, cooler altitudes of up to 6,560 ft (2,000 m).

● At night, chimps build nests 16–118 ft (5–36 m) high in the trees. In the rainy season, they also build day nests.

SOCIAL STRUCTURE

Chimpanzees are highly social animals, living in groups of anywhere from 15 to 125 individuals. Within these large groups there may exist smaller, more closely knit family groupings of between 3 and 6 individuals.

The group occupies a large territory, sometimes as great as 19 square miles (50 square kilometers), though individual chimpanzees tend to spend most of their time in an area as small as half a square mile (one square kilometer).

CLOSE-KNIT FAMILIES

The most common arrangement involves a group of about 4 or 5 unrelated females living in a territory dominated and defended by a small group of related males. Each female has her own territory, which overlaps with those of the other females.

Families remain close to each other, both physically and emotionally, throughout the chimps' relatively long lives. Chimpanzees are capable of reaching up to 50 years of age, though very old chimps are rarely seen in the wild, probably because elderly animals are easily caught and killed by predators. Similarly, if a chimpanzee becomes ill, it does not usually survive for long.

CHIMPS OFTEN TAKE NAPS DURING THE DAY AND WILL BUILD THEMSELVES SPECIAL BEDS IN THE TREES

Chimpanzees are mainly active during the daytime, rising with the dawn to set out in search of food. If they find a good source of food, such as a tree laden with strychnos fruit, several chimps may gather to gorge themselves on a large meal before resting and then moving on.

Despite their skill at climbing, most chimpanzees spend a good deal of their time on the ground. They usually "knuckle-walk" on all fours, but sometimes take several paces forward on their hind legs—when, for example, a male is displaying himself to a potential mate, or when carrying something with both hands.

NESTS IN THE TREES

At night, each adult normally makes itself a bed or nest of branches, twigs, and leaves where it will rest and sleep until the morning. In general, adults sleep alone, while mothers will cradle their young in the nest until they can fend for themselves. Sometimes

THE CHIMP'S TERRITORY

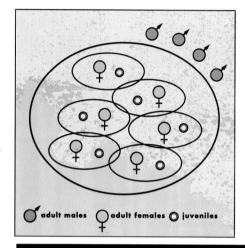

adult males adult females juveniles

Like most primates, chimps live in groups. These normally consist of a number of breeding females who live with their offspring within individual overlapping ranges. These in turn are situated within the territory of a few related adult males, who, consequently, hold a monopoly on the right to breed with the females.

FEMALE CHIMPS
(right) *may form strong links with other females in their group, especially if they are related, but they are usually more solitary than males.*

Illustrations John Cox/Wildlife Art Agency

SUBORDINATE
males (left) *perform important roles within the group, despite their inferior status. They form bonds with other males and set out with them on foraging expeditions.*

CHIMP GROUPS
Family relationships

CHIMPANZEES

have one of the longest maternal periods of any animal. They will stay with their mothers until they are about seven years of age.

THE DOMINANT

male (left) *may use occasional aggressive behavior to emphasize his authority and to remind other males of the group hierarchy.*

in SIGHT

FACIAL EXPRESSIONS

When it gets angry, the chimpanzee draws back its lips, fiercely baring both its top and bottom teeth *(left)*.

A chimp in a state of excitement will push its mobile lips forward to make a shape like a trumpet *(right)*.

Excitement relaxes the chimp's face into a grin as it makes an "oh-oh" sound that turns into a bark *(left)*.

The quiet expression and pursed lips of this chimpanzee denote a tranquil and concentrated mood *(right)*.

chimps will make themselves beds during the day as well if they want a nap. This is particularly common in young chimps, who may be practicing a skill they will need later on.

The daytime bed is simpler than the night bed, consisting of a crumpled mass of twigs, vines, and leaves. Male chimps make day beds less often than females, probably because males tend to be more actively on the lookout and therefore prefer to take their naps lying on the ground instead, where they can react more quickly to danger.

Chimpanzee groups regularly display territorial behavior, with rival groups making loud hooting noises at each other. From such behavior, each group gets an idea of the size of the other. If one is much smaller, the larger group may decide to take advantage of its strength in numbers and drive the smaller group away, though often the two sides back off after a noisy encounter.

Male chimpanzees establish power hierarchies, with a dominant older male as leader. Each individual knows its place, and subordinate males bob down or crouch when the dominant male approaches. Occasionally, the dominant male may charge others, hair erect to make him look even larger, possibly dragging along a branch as well. The dominant male remains in charge until successfully challenged by a stronger adult male.

VIOLENT ACTS

A typical display of aggression by a male chimpanzee to other males usually takes the following pattern: He stands up on his hind legs and sways from foot to foot with a sideways movement. He may then beat his chest, and his hair begins to stand out from his body. This makes him look even larger than he is. At this point the chimp may stoop toward the ground and beat it repeatedly with his hands. Then finally the creature picks up a branch and runs with it toward the other chimps.

Within the group, such displays rarely end in serious fights, and subordinate males usually cower before the dominant male. This may be followed by a bout of mutual grooming. One animal sits close to another and picks through its fur, pausing occasionally to pull off seeds or ticks and other parasites. Chimps certainly seem to enjoy these grooming sessions, which may help to cement the bonds between individuals and reduce aggression.

Grooming acts as a sign of acceptance and friendship, although, of course, it is practical as well.

NEST BUILDING

Helmut Albrecht/Bruce Coleman Ltd.

Each individual chimp builds a fresh tree nest every night in close proximity to the group. Nests are usually built in one of a number of favored locations, safe from predators. The nest consists of a base of branches some 15 feet (4.5 meters) up, into which twigs are woven.

When they are about one year old, young chimps help in the construction of the nest they share with their mother, learning these essential skills by imitating her actions.

A WEAPON,

such as this stick, may be used by an aggressive male and waved in a threatening gesture. Alternatively, he may beat his chest.

AGGRESSION

is often signaled by stamping on or slapping the ground. This may lead to the aggressive chimp charging at the others.

Illustrations John Cox/Wildlife Art Agency

Chimpanzees also embrace, pat, hold hands, and kiss, as a greeting or to give comfort.

Despite these displays of affection, the image of chimpanzees as peaceful vegetarians is far from the truth, and cases of murder, infanticide, and cannibalism are not uncommon. Occasionally, large parties of up to forty males are formed, usually when food is abundant, on the edges of two territorial groups. Smaller groups act as patrols, checking the borders and gauging the strength of the neighboring group. If they find a male who has wandered away from this group, they may chase, ambush and injure, or even kill him.

DESPITE DISPLAYS OF AFFECTION, CASES OF MURDER, INFANTICIDE, AND EVEN CANNIBALISM OCCUR

A female with young babies strays into a neighboring territory at great peril. Local males will recognize her as foreign and may attack and kill her young, sometimes eating them as well. It should be emphasized that incidents such as these tend to occur during periods of unusual risk taking associated with migration and increasing population density.

A SIMPLE LANGUAGE

Chimps in the wild make a variety of sounds, ranging from loud grunts to whoops and shrieks, and some mean particular things to other chimpanzees. Loud hooting cries echo through the forest, and chimps can recognize individuals by the pattern or tone of hoot. They also scream when in pain or under attack, and this brings relatives rushing to help. On the other hand, they can be silent for long periods, just muttering soft grunts. ■

WHEN A LONE MALE APPROACHES,

males from a group will use threatening gestures, chase him, and finally attack him—some of the chimps will beat him and bite him, while others hold him down. Males often form border patrols, protecting the boundaries of their community's territory from invaders and other groups.

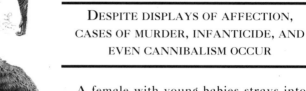

A SUBORDINATE MALE

bobs and grunts before another male chimpanzee, acknowledging the dominant status of his rival.

KEY FACTS

● Most chimpanzees spend up to 80 percent of their time within a range of only 0.4–1.9 sq mi (1–5 sq km).

● Male chimps rarely leave the community in which they were born. Females, by contrast, migrate to other groups as soon as they are old enough to breed.

● Unlike common chimp groups, pygmy chimp groups usually contain equal numbers of males and females.

FOOD AND FEEDING

Chimpanzees are well suited to their forest or savanna homes and make the most of the abundant food resources they provide. Though they roam as a group, they normally search for their own food. There are exceptions to this, however, such as when several gather at a fruit tree. Even then, the chimps tend to arrive individually and compete for their share. Chimpanzees eat fruit for at least four or five hours each day, and, along with young, newly sprouted leaves, it makes up most of their diet.

CONSTANT FORAGING

Moving through the forest in search of a good supply of food, chimps will settle down to a heavy meal before retiring for a nap of an hour or two—after which they will be ready for their next meal. They do not need to gather and store food, because forest resources are available all year-round.

In areas where chimpanzees live outside the

FORAGING

Chimpanzees are largely vegetarian, with up to 90 percent of their diet consisting of ripe fruits (right). *In areas with a marked dry period, chimps will also eat the seeds of trees, bark, resin, pith, and flowers.*

Illustrations Chris Turnbull/Wildlife Art Agency

Steve Robinson/NHPA

TOOL USE

The chimpanzee's precise manipulative skills are made possible by its grasping thumb. This, combined with surprising intellectual capabilities, means chimps are one of the few mammals with the ability to use tools. A chimp will push thin sticks or blades of grass into an ant or termite nest, and, when the insects attack the stick, the chimp will pull it out and eat the insects clinging to it.

The chimpanzee's tool kit includes hard stones or rocks for smashing open the tough shells of certain fruits, wooden clubs that are used to smash nuts against tree trunks, makeshift sponges fashioned from a bundle of leaves or chewed bark, and bunches of twigs with leaves that function as flyswatters.

forest, in grassland or savanna habitats, they can migrate over quite long distances—covering areas of up to 155 square miles (400 square kilometers)—in order to ensure a good supply of food. Each time they find a reliable food supply, they settle down for several weeks or more until that supply is exhausted, then move on again.

TASTY MORSELS

Although largely vegetarian, chimpanzees will also eat insects such as termites, ants, and caterpillars. Termites are nutritious and can be found in huge numbers in their colonies. Once a colony has been found, it is easy for a chimp to make a good meal at one sitting.

Chimpanzees, especially males, occasionally eat birds and hunt for mammals. In Tanzania's Gombe

NIMBLE FINGERS

Chimpanzees sometimes use tools to help get at their food—grass stems or small sticks are useful for coaxing insects like termites and ants out of their nests.

In the Ivory Coast's Tai Forest, chimpanzees hunt adult monkeys in a gang of about six (right). One or two adult males chase the monkeys through the trees, while others block their escape routes—then one male goes in for the kill.

Illustration Matt Lyon

THIRSTY WORK

Chimps rarely need to drink water because they obtain the moisture from the fruit and leaves they consume.

Although chimps are mainly vegetarian, they will also eat birds, insects, and mammals such as bushpig, monkeys, and antelope.

COLOBUS MONKEY

SITATUNGA

BUSHPIG

National Park, where the favorite prey is the red colobus monkey, chimps chase young monkeys in an uncoordinated way and surprise and kill them when they become separated from their mothers; they may even tear the mother-and-baby pair apart. Hunting methods vary among chimp populations. In the Tai Forest of the Ivory Coast, for example, gangs of males cooperate in the kill.

On a more peaceful note, chimpanzees have been seen collecting and slowly chewing the leaves of a certain herb, aspilia, in the Gombe National Park. The herb has no obvious food value to the chimpanzees, but it does contain a powerful natural antibiotic. It seems likely that chimpanzees seek out this herb as a natural medicine when they are feeling ill. ■

Illustrations Ruth Grewcock

LIFE CYCLE

I n the wild, female chimps start to breed when they
are about 12 years old, though they will mate only
when they are in heat, which happens about every
four to six weeks. This condition lasts for two or
three weeks, during which time the pink skin of her
rear swells as a signal that she is ready to mate. A
female in heat may mate several times a day, and the
males compete for the right to mate with her.

HELPLESS BABIES

Usually, a receptive female forms a pair bond with
a single dominant male toward the end of this
period, and the two will tend to keep away from
other chimpanzees at this time. It is during this time
that the female is most likely to conceive, and, by
keeping her clear of rival males, the dominant male
insures that he will be the father of her offspring.
After about 235 days a single baby is born. Though
on rare occasions twins may be produced, their
survival prospects in the wild are poor.

ALTHOUGH A FEMALE CHIMP IS OFTEN
FERTILE FOR A LONG TIME—ABOUT 25
YEARS—SHE IS LIKELY TO PRODUCE NO
MORE THAN FIVE YOUNG IN HER LIFETIME

Newborn chimps are almost wholly dependent
on their mother. They cling to her belly fur, and this
remains their favored position until they are about
five months old, after which they start to ride
piggyback. By the age of three, young chimps are

AMAZING FACTS

PHYSICAL FEATS

**Although chimpanzees are usually gentle,
an adult male chimpanzee, with its broad
muscular chest and strong arms, has the
strength of three men and is capable of
considerable feats. During fights or
territorial disputes, it can pick up and hurl
large boulders or branches at rivals with
seeming ease.**

**A group of males attacking an intruder
or making a foray into alien territory is a
frightening sight. They can kill other animals
by smashing them against the ground or by
stamping on them, and inflict terrible
wounds using their sharp canine teeth.**

GROWING UP
The life of a young chimpanzee

BABY CHIMPANZEES

*are helpless; they remain
dependent on their
mothers for up to
seven or eight
years, though
weaning occurs
during the
third year.*

MALE CHIMPS BEGIN

*exhibiting sexual behaviors
toward females at three to four
years of age but do not reach
puberty until about seven. Males
do not attain full integration
into normal social hierarchy
until midteens.*

YOUNG MALES FIGHT

*for dominance. Their
displays include chases,
physical attacks—hitting or
stamping—and screaming.*

YOUNG CHIMPS RIDE

on their mothers' backs as soon as they are able, at around five to seven months. By the time they are four years old, they will travel mostly by walking alongside their mothers.

CHIMPS PLAY

with other young chimps and with their mothers from the age of about eight months.

Illustrations Chris Turnbull/Wildlife Art Agency

Gerry Ellis/Nature Photography

LOOK AND LEARN

Just like children, chimps learn a great deal by imitating older chimps, which is a much more efficient process in terms of the species' survival than trial and error. Living in groups gives chimps an excellent opportunity to watch and learn from others, so new tricks and techniques can be passed on to the next generation. Sometimes special skills are developed within particular groups.

Young chimps also learn through play. Like many young mammals they indulge in mock fights and tumbles, safely honing the skills which they will later use for real in hunting and fighting. Young chimpanzees start to prepare sticks at the age of two or three and use these in their play. Later, they will copy their elders and use them to fish for ants and termites.

weaned, but they are not fully independent until they reach about seven or eight. A female is able to conceive and produce offspring for about twenty-five years, though in practice she usually has no more than about five young during her lifetime.

Male chimpanzees are sexually very precocious. They begin mounting females by the time they are two years old, but they do not establish their full courtship rituals until they reach the age of about four. Then they will grab the attention of a receptive female by shaking branches, stripping leaves from trees, and standing near to her with their hair erect. If the female is ready to mate, she adopts a squatting posture in front of the male, who then mounts her from behind.

The behavior of pygmy chimps is less well known, as they are rare and therefore difficult to study. However, recent research has shown them to be even more sexually active, at all ages, than common chimpanzees. Pygmy chimps also show great variety in their sexual exploits, and, unlike common chimps, they sometimes mate face-to-face. They even seem to kiss each other in a very human way.

SEXUAL PROMISCUITY

Pygmy females remain sexually active throughout most of their pregnancy and when feeding their young. This extended period of sexual activity is another attribute chimps share with humans. It is yet undetermined, but increased sexual activity might contribute in some way to social bonding and overall group cohesion.

To date, scientists have no clear idea why these distinctive behavioral differences should exist between two such closely related species. ∎

OUR PROFIT, THEIR LOSS

HUMANS ARE THE MAIN ENEMY OF AFRICA'S CHIMPS. IN THEIR NATURAL HOMES, THEY ARE UNDER THREAT AS NEVER BEFORE AS A RESULT OF HABITAT DESTRUCTION, ILLEGAL TRAPPING, AND LOCAL PERSECUTION

In recent decades, chimpanzees have declined rapidly across the whole of their natural range. Many of the populations that still remain are small and separated. These isolated populations can easily be wiped out by an epidemic; they may also experience an increase in inbreeding, eventually leading to an inability to adapt to their surroundings. This means that—unless firm action is taken to protect them—these populations will, undoubtedly, be pushed to extinction.

TAKING OVER

At the heart of the problem is the rapid increase in human populations in many African countries—the more people there are, the less room there is for local wildlife. The human population in Zaire, Gabon, and Guinea has been estimated to be as high as 300 million and it is increasing at a rate of about 3 percent a year. Competition for land and forest resources among humans results in loss of habitat for chimpanzees. Their forest homes are being

---

HUMAN EXPANSION IN CENTRAL AFRICAN COUNTRIES IS DISPLACING LOCAL CHIMP POPULATIONS AS THE TREES ARE FELLED FOR COMMERCIAL LOGGING

---

destroyed at an alarming rate as trees are cut down for their timber or cleared to provide land for agriculture, grazing, or housing.

At the end of the 19th century, the tropical forests of West Africa covered about 162,000 square miles (420,000 square kilometers). Today only about 63,700 square miles (165,000 square kilometers) of forest are left, which means that about two-thirds have been destroyed in the last hundred years. In Guinea, Ivory Coast, and Sierra Leone, for example, only about 10

percent of the original forest cover remains.

Once chimpanzees could be found throughout most of the tropical parts of Africa, in twenty-five countries stretching from southern Senegal to western Tanzania. Now the picture is very different, and all that remain are pockets of chimpanzee populations in about half of these countries.

GLOOMY FORECASTS

The total chimpanzee population in the wild may now be as low as 200,000, a drop of some 50,000—one quarter of the population—since the 1980s. Most are to be found in Gabon, Zaire, and Guinea. In Gabon there were an estimated 64,000 wild chimps in the early 1980s. More recent estimates project that by 1996 the numbers of chimpanzees there may have dropped to less than 50,000.

The greatest threat to chimpanzees is the destruction of the environment. Trade, on a much lesser scale, is also a problem.

THEN & NOW

The charts below show the worldwide uses of exported chimpanzees in 1981 and in 1991. The shaded areas represent the trade in captive-bred chimps.

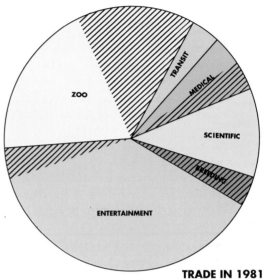

TRADE IN 1981

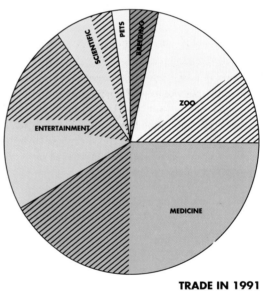

TRADE IN 1991

⬛ **CAPTIVE-BRED CHIMPANZEES**

In the 1980s, the use of chimps in our society changed to suit our needs.

● In 1981, chimps were mainly exported to zoos and sold for commercial uses.

● Trade figures from 1991 show that chimps traded to zoos and the entertainment industry shrank, while medical research increased (except in the United States).

Although they are not as great a threat as the loss of habitat, poachers have also contributed to the chimp's decline. Modern weapons are now freely available in many countries, especially where there is war and political unrest, and these are all too frequently turned on chimpanzees by poachers intent on earning cold, hard cash.

CRUEL SLAUGHTER

The modern hunter, equipped with powerful automatic firearms, can easily pick off all the adults in a group of chimpanzees. Other barbaric methods used to kill adults protecting their young include poisoning and the use of dogs, nets, and traps. The bodies of the adults are traded locally as food, while the young are taken away and sold for export.

For every young chimpanzee caught in the wild, between ten and thirty others may have been killed. For example, in Sierra Leone, official records show that 3,000 young chimpanzees were exported in

---

CHIMP DEFENSES ARE NO MATCH FOR POACHERS' BULLETS. THE SUFFERING CONTINUES FOR THE INFANT SURVIVORS AS THEY ARE TRANSPORTED ABROAD

---

twenty years. This means that at least 30,000 others must have died—and almost certainly many more, since many kidnappings would have gone undetected. Trade in great apes has come under strict regulation or outright ban. This has tremendously helped diminish these tragedies.

After their capture, the helpless infant chimpanzees begin a nightmare journey of physical and mental suffering. They are often tied hand and foot and transported in trucks to holding pens at ports or airports. Then they begin their journey overseas, often under conditions of great discomfort. Many die on the way, from dehydration or disease, or soon after their arrival, from the long-term effects of their ordeal. The survivors are sold abroad as pets, as entertainers in circuses, or as "guinea pigs" for medical research.

FINDING A CURE

Chimpanzees are widely used in medical research, especially in the United States and Europe. Because they are so closely related to people, chimps can catch many human diseases such as hepatitis and may also be infected with HIV (human immunodeficiency virus), which causes the disease AIDS (acquired immunodeficiency syndrome).

The demand for wild chimps by laboratories has increased in the last few years as scientists race to find a cure for this dread disease. New vaccines are

Tim Laman/Wildlife Collection

ENDANGERED SPECIES

THE TRADE IN WILDLIFE: CRUELTY TO CHIMPANZEES

☐ MAIN EXPORTING COUNTRIES

While much of the trade in wildlife is strictly controlled by legislation, more than a third is illegal—where endangered species are taken from the wild and smuggled overseas.

The demand for chimps is great, particularly from laboratories: Researchers will pay $25,000 for an infant chimp. The main importers are the United States, Japan, and continental Europe.

DEFYING THE AUTHORITIES

The trade in wild chimps is thriving. Infant chimps captured in Liberia and Guinea are smuggled into Sierra Leone to be shipped abroad, even though exports from there have been banned since 1978. Illegal exports from Uganda, Zaire, and Tanzania are on the increase.

Baby chimps are wholly dependent on their mothers and many die as a result of the trauma of being captured. Their chances of survival may also be reduced because of infection by human diseases, or improper feeding by handlers.

Fearful of a strange environment, young chimps suffer high levels of stress when separated from one another. They are also severely affected by extremes in

CONSERVATION MEASURES

With increased public awareness, the suffering of chimps should be alleviated.

● The International Air Transport Association (IATA) has produced live-animal regulations for transporting wildlife. So far 19 countries have recognized them.

● TRAFFIC (Trade Records Analysis of

temperature—wind or drafts can be fatal, and exposure to direct heat or sunlight will lead to dehydration. The mortality rate among exported chimps may be as high as 50 percent.

Stress caused during transportation can have prolonged effects, even after the animals have arrived at their destination. For example, all nine chimps illegally imported into Austria in 1982 died within weeks of arrival, despite attempts to rehabilitate them by the Vienna Zoo. Even if the traumatized young chimps survive the journey, they are often in need of intensive medical care.

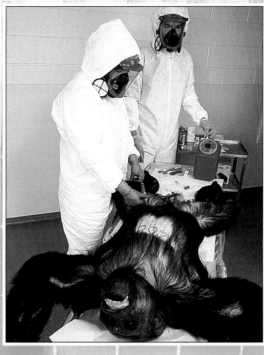

Michael K. Nichols/Magnum Photos

A BLOOD SAMPLE IS TAKEN FROM A CHIMPANZEE'S THIGH IN A NEW YORK MEDICAL LABORATORY.

Flora and Fauna in Commerce) monitors world trade in animals and plants, intercepting illegal activities.

● Almost all countries with primate populations now control export in some way. The United States refuses the entry of any primates that have been exported from another country illegally, and all primate imports as pets have been banned since 1975 because of viruses.

CHIMPANZEES IN DANGER

THE CHART BELOW SHOWS HOW THE INTERNATIONAL UNION FOR THE CONSERVATION OF NATURE (IUCN), OR THE WORLD CONSERVATION UNION, CLASSIFIES THE STATUS OF CHIMPANZEES:

WEST AFRICAN CHIMPANZEE	ENDANGERED
OTHER COMMON CHIMPANZEES	VULNERABLE
PYGMY CHIMPANZEE	VULNERABLE

ENDANGERED MEANS THAT THE ANIMAL IS IN DANGER OF EXTINCTION AND ITS SURVIVAL IS UNLIKELY UNLESS STEPS ARE TAKEN TO SAVE IT. *VULNERABLE* INDICATES THAT THE ANIMAL IS LIKELY TO MOVE INTO THE ENDANGERED CATEGORY IF THINGS CONTINUE AS THEY ARE.

Philip Steele/ICCE Photolibrary

tested on the chimps in the hope that their bodies will react in a similar way to ours.

About 3,000 chimps are held in captivity in the United States, of which around 2,000 are kept in labs, 500 in zoos, and 500 in the entertainment industry. In 1990 about 1,300 were used in biomedical research labs.

TRAFFICKING IN LIVE CHIMPANZEES CONTINUES, DESPITE THE INTRODUCTION OF INTERNATIONAL LAWS PROHIBITING THEIR EXPORT

Chimps such as these can be taken from the wild only by special agreement. As they are an endangered species, there are strict laws prohibiting the export of live chimpanzees, though it is extremely difficult to enforce these laws on the ground, and illegal trafficking continues. Outside the United States, another 2,000 chimps are in captivity. Their plight varies from being experimented upon in laboratories to being held captive in zoos, menageries, or entertainment parks.

LIMITED SUPPLIES

The demand for chimpanzees from the wild could be stemmed by finding successful breeding programs in captivity. However, so far laboratories and researchers have had only limited success in breeding their own supply of animals.

Chimpanzees breed well only in zoos or parks that closely mimic their natural environment. Even

493

ALONGSIDE MAN

TOURIST RESORTS

Every year many visitors to Spain's major tourist resorts pose for photographs with baby chimps. Engaging though they may be, these chimps are victims of a cruel and illegal trade. They are often shot full of powerful debilitating drugs and forced to parade their pathetic affections for anywhere up to 16 hours a day.

The WWF is now leading a campaign to make tourists aware of this appalling practice, though, so far, the Spanish authorities seem unwilling to comply.

Michael K. Nichols/Magnum Photos

if their chimps do breed successfully, the wildlife park wardens, who place a high value on preserving a happy colony of animals, naturally would not wish to donate their young chimps to medical research and a life of abject misery.

A DIFFICULT PROCESS

Some chimpanzees are rescued or confiscated from illegal traders, hunters, and importers. However, they present formidable problems for the conservationists who attempt to rehabilitate them in sanctuaries.

This process is fraught with difficulties. The confiscated chimps may have been too affected by the traumas they have suffered in captivity to take to the wild again. Alternatively, they may have become too accustomed to being with people to respond properly to their own kind. They will not have learned to hunt for and gather their own food and may not be able to find enough to eat if they are released back into the wild.

Having been imported illegally, baby chimps are often used as photographers' "clowns" in Spanish resorts.

Far from their forest homes, chimps are a popular pet in many countries, at the mercy of their owners.

If rescued chimpanzees are released into an area with established chimpanzees, they are likely to be attacked and even killed. One answer is to create sanctuaries for the rescued animals. There are now several successful centers for housing chimpanzees in a nearly wild state, such as those run by the Jane Goodall Institute. Sanctuaries run under this scheme have been set up in Kenya, Burundi, Gambia, Zambia, Congo, the United States, and Britain, and plans are under way for a new sanctuary in

> ONE SOLUTION TO THE PROBLEM OF REHABILITATING RESCUED CHIMPS IS TO CREATE SANCTUARIES WHERE ANIMALS LIVE A NEARLY WILD EXISTENCE

Glasgow. However, the very scale of the problem means that many more such centers are needed.

In their natural environment, chimpanzees thrive in a wide range of habitats and it is essential that these are maintained. Several reserves have already been set up in countries with large populations of chimpanzees, but a range of woodland and savanna habitats must also be protected to conserve isolated populations.

Fortunately, controlled tourism programs are now being set up all over Africa. These can provide additional income and incentives to local people to conserve native chimpanzees. Wildlife tourists are charged a fee to visit wild chimpanzee colonies under the careful guidance and supervision of local wardens. The proceeds can then be fed back into the local conservation initiative to benefit the animals. In the Salonga National Park in Zaire, for example, groups of pygmy chimpanzees are unwittingly boosting local tourism while being protected in their natural habitat. ∎

Michael K. Nichols/Magnum Photos

INTO THE FUTURE

At present rates of loss, both the common and the pygmy chimp may be extinct in the wild within the 21st century, or even sooner. Without more extensive research, though, it will be difficult to estimate exactly how isolated populations will fare in remote areas or in dense forest in the next few years.

Even in the largest areas of prime tropical forest, such as those of Gabon and northern Zaire, there may be fewer wild chimpanzees than we think. These current chimp strongholds are being increasingly affected by logging by the timber industry and by clearance for agriculture and land development programs.

Wild chimpanzees can be really sure of survival only in areas that are controlled and well protected, such as national parks and other nature preserves. One successful preserve is the Gombe National Park in Tanzania, where the chimp population should continue to be healthy in numbers if

PREDICTION

TRAFFIC SEIZURES

The continued seizures of wild animals by TRAFFIC is likely to make life more difficult for chimp smugglers in the future. Any offenders caught are usually forced to pay a heavy fine. In 1991, a total of eleven illegally imported chimps were rescued from circus trainers in Europe alone.

conditions remain favorable.

Outside the preserves the endless pressures and disturbances from humans are taking their toll and, in some areas, are pushing the species toward the brink of extinction. It would be a huge tragedy if we caused the disappearance of our own closest relative, perhaps within our own lifetimes.

A SHELTERED EXISTENCE

The good news is that, in a number of key areas, new preserves have been created to help conserve chimpanzees, and more are being planned. The Salonga National Park in Zaire now protects a thriving population of pygmy chimpanzees. The Gombe Park has only about 150 chimpanzees, but now a second area, the Mahale Mountains National Park, has been created where there is a population of about 700. ∎

CHIMPANZOO

Chimpanzoo is an American initiative that aims to improve the life of chimpanzees in captivity. It was set up by Jane Goodall, who has devoted most of her adult life to studying chimps in the wild. Several zoos throughout the United States are now involved in the program, including Cheyenne Mountain Zoo in Colorado Springs, North Carolina Zoo, Washington Park Zoo, and San Francisco Zoo.

Chimpanzoo is a network of zoos and wildlife parks that enables researchers to make close studies of chimp behavior. Scientists recommend to the zoos ways of keeping the animals that closely mimic their natural habitats.

As zoo managers realize how inventive chimpanzees can be, they are changing the ways in which they house them. Increasingly, captive chimps have access to interesting and stimulating environments.

HUMAN RIGHTS

There is now a widely held view among conservationists that chimpanzees and other great apes should be given the same moral status as ourselves. According to this view, it should be illegal to kill any of the great apes (except in self-defense), keep them in captivity, use them in medical research, or subject them to any form of pain or suffering.

This argument is based on the similarities between apes and humans. Molecular evidence suggests that we share 98.4 percent of our DNA—the molecules that are responsible for passing on genetic characteristics from parent to offspring—with chimpanzees, proving that they are our closest living relatives.

CIVETS

RELATIONS

The civets and genets are members of the family Viverridae. Other viverrid species include:

DWARF MONGOOSES

EGYPTIAN MONGOOSES

GRAY MEERKAT

Nick Gordon/Ardea

PRIMITIVE PREDATORS

MEMBERS OF THE LARGEST FAMILY OF CARNIVORES, CIVETS AND GENETS
ARE NEVERTHELESS AMONG THE MOST POORLY KNOWN AND LEAST
STUDIED OF ANIMALS IN THIS GROUP

There are some seventy-one species in the family Viverridae of civets, genets, mongooses, and their relatives; together they make up the largest family of carnivores. All are found only in the Old World, having never invaded the New World, and they live mainly in tropical and southern temperate areas.

Like all carnivores, civets and genets originated in the Eocene epoch (54–38 million years ago). The superfamily that existed at this time and which gave rise to all subsequent carnivores was the Miacoidea, which were fairly small forest-dwellers with short legs and spreading paws. Fossils of the earliest viverrids show resemblances to the earliest species in the Miacoidea superfamily and some authorities claim several of the modern species to be nothing more than advanced miacids. Certainly genets and civets are among the most primitive of living carnivores, and their teeth and skeletons have changed little over the past 40–50 million years.

CLASSIFICATION

Together with the mongooses, the 71 species of civet and genet belong to the Viverridae family in the carnivore order.

ORDER

Carnivora
(carnivores)

FAMILY

Viverridae
(civets, genets, mongooses)

SUBFAMILY

Viverrinae
(true civets, genets, linsangs)
19 species in 7 genera

SUBFAMILY

Paradoxurinae
(palm civets)
8 species in 6 genera

SUBFAMILY

Hemigalinae
(palm civets, otter civets)
5 species in 4 genera

SUBFAMILY

Euplerinae
(falanouc)
1 species

SUBFAMILY

Cryptoproctinae
(fossa)
1 species

SUBFAMILY

Fossinae
(fanaloka)
1 species

497

Of the modern carnivore families the viverrids were among the earliest to appear, and from them originated two other groups—the hyenas (hyaenids) and the cats (felids). The cats diverged toward the end of the Eocene epoch, while modern hyenas originated around 24 million years ago.

CIVETS AND GENETS TODAY

Today, civets and genets are contained in six subfamilies, three of which occur only in Madagascar and have only one species each. Of the remaining three the Paradoxurinae, or palm civets, are found mainly in southern Asia; of its eight species, only one —the African palm civet—is found in Africa. Within this group is the largest of all the viverrids discussed here—the binturong, whose shaggy form is almost more bearlike than catlike. Like a bear, its claws are nonretractile, and it walks on its soles rather than on its toes (like a dog); most civets and genets are similarly "flat-footed." Unusually, its long tail has a prehensile tip, for this animal is almost entirely arboreal, moving slowly among the trees, wrapping its tail around a branch and letting go only when it has a firm grip with its feet. Other species in this group resemble the genets and linsangs to some extent, although they tend to be heavier bodied.

The largest of the subfamilies is the Viverrinae, which contains 19 species known as the true civets, the linsangs, and the genets. The African civet is the best known and vies with the large Indian civet for the title of the biggest. There are five true civets in all. The three species of linsang—the banded, spotted, and African—are among the most beautiful of all viverrids, but they are also among the shyest and least known—probably among the rarest, too. There are 11 species of genet, the most widespread of which, the common genet, is the only one of its kind to have colonized Europe, although some authorities think it was originally introduced there by humans.

The remaining subfamily, the Hemigalinae, contains the banded palm and otter civets and has five species. These are all inhabitants of the rain forests of Southeast Asia and the best known is the banded palm civet. The otter civets, as their name suggests, are extremely aquatic, although they are also agile climbers. Adaptations to a watery lifestyle include nostrils that open upward on the top of the muzzle and may be closed by flaps, ears that can also be closed, long, plentiful whiskers for detecting prey underwater, and a particularly dense coat comprising a close underfur topped by longer, coarse guard hairs that help repel water. The feet are only partially webbed—and not to the extent found in true otters.

The genets have evolved into a wide range of woodland predators with "dazzle" camouflage.

Gerard Lacz/NHPA

in SIGHT

MADAGASCANS

Three viverrids in this group have evolved separately from all others in the rarefied island environment of Madagascar. These are the fossa, the fanaloka, and the falanouc.

The fossa, *Cryptoprocta ferox,* is Madagascar's largest native carnivore *(above).* It looks rather like a small puma, but is also similar to mongooses and civets. It lives in the trees in dense rain forest.

The much smaller fanaloka, or Malagasy civet, *Fossa fossa,* is more foxy in appearance. Its short, fine coat is a pale gray to reddish brown marked with rows of darker spots that almost merge into stripes. It has short, slender legs with nonretractile claws. In many ways the fanaloka resembles the true civets but it lacks the anal scent glands. Unusual among these animals, it tends to live in pairs.

The falanouc, *Eupleres goudoti,* is terrestrial but entirely solitary. It lacks the striped and spotted markings of the fanaloka, instead having a coat that is beige on the back and sides and paler on the undersides. Its tail is rather bushy. The falanouc is unusual in storing fat in the root of the tail at times when food is plentiful.

The viverrids found in Africa evolved and developed alongside a number of other carnivores, most of them larger and extremely efficient at hunting and killing. As a result, African viverrids tend to occupy the small carnivore niches, usually living in concealed habitats, hunting by night, and preying on small animals. Their Asian counterparts evolved in an area which, by and large, contained far fewer carnivore species, so they were more able to diversify into a wider variety of niches.

PROTECTIVE PATTERNING

Most of the viverrids discussed here display elaborate coat markings of spots, blotches, or stripes. Many have tails that are as long as their bodies and that may be ringed in alternate light and dark bands. As with all animal coloration, the primary function is concealment, important in these animals to hide them from both predators and prey. Markings and coat colorings will tend, therefore, to vary according to location. Those species found in arid, semidesert areas generally have paler, sand-colored coats, while the forest or woodland species tend to be darker, with broken markings of spots or blotches that make them hard to pick out against a background of mottled light and shade. ■

THE VIVERRIDS' FAMILY TREE

Civets and genets are contained in the order Carnivora, which includes cats, dogs, hyenas, bears, raccoons, coatis and pandas, martens, badgers, skunks, otters, seals, sea lions and walruses, as well as the mongooses, which are the civets' and genets' closest relatives. The cats and hyenas are sometimes included with the viverrids within a superfamily known as the viverrids.

FOSSA
Cryptoprocta ferox
(*krip-to-PROCK-tah FEH-rocks*)

The fossa is the only species in the subfamily Cryptoproctinae. The largest of Madagascar's native carnivores, it is considered to be the ecological equivalent of the clouded leopard of Southeast Asia. Even though it is plantigrade (walks on its soles), it has completely retractile claws on each foot.

BANDED PALM CIVET
Hemigalus derbyanus
(*hemmy-GAH-lus der-be-AHN-us*)

An inhabitant of Southeast Asian islands, this slender palm civet has a yellowish-buff coat with darker stripes across its back and sides. These stop about a third of the way down the tail. The pointed face has striped markings, and dark patches encircle the eyes.

VIVERRIDAE

WEASELS

RACCOONS

BEARS

DOGS

DOGLIKE CARNIVORES

COMMON SPOTTED GENET
Genetta genetta
(jen-ETT-ah jen-ETT-ah)

This slim, catlike viverrid has long, coarse fur marked with spots on the upper parts and flanks. The long tail has nine or ten narrower rings. The back hairs are longer along the genet's spine, forming a prominent crest of "hackles" that may be erected when the animal is angry or threatened.

The African palm civet is somewhat chunky in appearance, with a short, woolly coat that is usually a gray brown tinged with red and sometimes displaying faint cream-colored spots, particularly between the shoulders. The long tail has indistinct rings and may be darker in color.

AFRICAN PALM CIVET
Nandinia binotata
(nan-DIN-ee-ah bin-o-TAH-tah)

MONGOOSES

CATS

HYENAS

CATLIKE CARNIVORES

ALL CARNIVORES

ANATOMY:

THE AFRICAN CIVET

THE DORSAL CREST

of dark hairs up to 4.5 in (11 cm) long runs along the spine into the tail. The civet erects this when threatened. It will often also turn sideways to appear more impressive to its attacker.

THE COAT

is heavily marked with stripes, spots, and blotches, which vary according to location. They provide the civet with camouflage.

The African civet (above left) has an average head-and-body length of 34 in (86 cm) but may reach 42 in (107 cm) and weigh up to 31 lb (14 kg). The little African linsang (above right) has an average head-and-body length of 13 in (33 cm), and weighs 21–23 oz (595–652 g). The binturong (above center) reaches about 32 in (81 cm) from head to rump.

GENET FORE

CIVET FORE

GENET HIND

CIVET HIND

FEET

In all species of civet and genet each foot has five toes, with semiretractile, fairly blunt claws. The genet's soles are hairy, whereas the African palm civet has naked feet to provide a grip on branches.

THE HEAD

has blunt, raccoonlike features; the snout is white and there is a black mask around the eyes. The ears are oval and conspicuous.

X

R A Y

CIVET SKELETON

The hindquarters are higher and more powerful than the forequarters. The effective length of the legs is increased by semidigitigrade or digitigrade posture. The rib cage is relatively shallow.

shallow rib cage

long tail for balance in trees

broad molars

CIVET

long, narrow skull

X-ray illustrations Elisabeth Smith

PALM CIVET

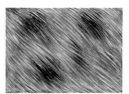

Sandy-brown coat with muted, indistinct dark blotches for camouflage.

BINTURONG

Dark, lustrous coat, often with gray, buff, or tawny tips to hairs.

BANDED LINSANG

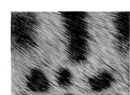

Pale, gray-brown coat with banded back and tail and spots on flanks.

CLASSIFICATION

GENUS: *CIVETTICTIS*

SPECIES: *CIVETTA*

SIZE

HEAD–BODY LENGTH: **26–35 IN (66–88 CM)**

TAIL LENGTH: APPROX. **20 IN (51 CM)**

HEIGHT TO SHOULDER: **13–15 IN (33–38 CM)**

WEIGHT: **15–44 LB (7–20 KG)**

MALES ARE LARGER THAN FEMALES

COLORATION

DARK SPOTS, STRIPES, AND BLOTCHES ON A GRAYISH OR TAWNY-BROWN BACKGROUND

LEGS AND TAIL ARE DARK

FACE HAS A RACCOONLIKE MASK, WITH WHITE MUZZLE AND SPECKLED GRAY FOREHEAD

FEATURES

RACCOONLIKE FACE MASK

HINDQUARTERS HIGHER THAN FOREQUARTERS

BLUNT, SEMIRETRACTILE CLAWS

DORSAL CREST OF ERECTILE, LONG DARK HAIRS

LARGE ANAL-SAC AND PERINEAL GLANDS UNDER TAIL

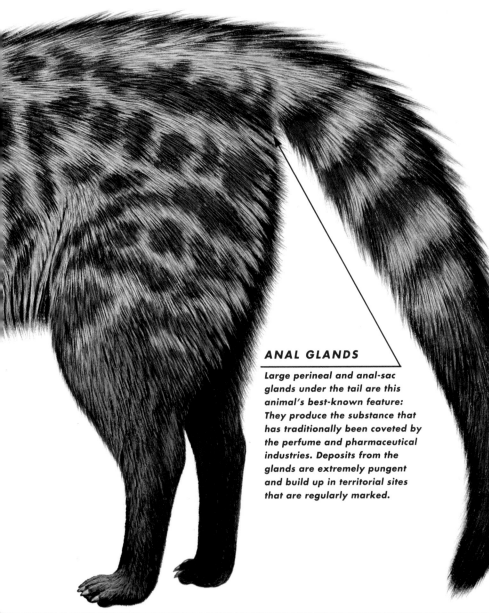

ANAL GLANDS

Large perineal and anal-sac glands under the tail are this animal's best-known feature: They produce the substance that has traditionally been coveted by the perfume and pharmaceutical industries. Deposits from the glands are extremely pungent and build up in territorial sites that are regularly marked.

THE TAIL

is broad at the base, tapering toward the tip. It measures perhaps a third of the animal's total length.

GENET

CIVET AND GENET SKULLS

The skull is remarkably strong and robust, although the cranium is long and narrow; it measures 6 in (15 cm) from front to back. The muzzle, too, is narrow. Civets have 40 teeth—10 more than is usual in cats; the molars are large and broad, similar to those of a dog.

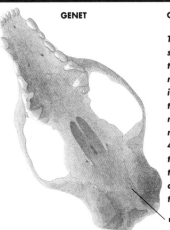

robust cranium

CIVET

GENET

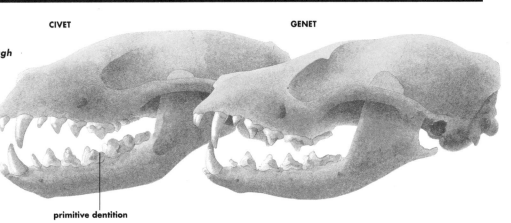

primitive dentition

Main illustration Simon Turvey/Wildlife Art Agency

ALONE IN THE DARK

THE CIVETS AND GENETS ARE SOLITARY, NOCTURNAL ANIMALS; NONE HAVE THE COMPLEX SOCIAL STRUCTURE OFTEN DISPLAYED BY THEIR CLOSE RELATIVES, THE MONGOOSES

T he lifestyle of all animals is dictated principally by their environment and their dietary requirements. Although civets and genets occupy a variety of ecological niches, they all depend on opportunistic foraging, generally using stealth to capture their prey. The small size of most viverrids means they are also likely to fall prey themselves, so they must always be alert—and remain hidden whenever possible. This means that a solitary life, in which the main activity occurs nocturnally, ensures the best chance of survival.

UNDER COVER OF NIGHT

Nevertheless, periods of activity do vary between species. Genets, for example, may be active during the day in the rainy season, while the African palm civet appears to have a period of high activity for about four hours after dusk, followed by a rest and another active period around dawn. This is because its favorite prey, birds and monkeys, tend to be at rest at these times and so are easy victims. The common genet in its European range is active mainly from sunset to dawn, with a resting period at some stage during the night. Daytime activity occurs only if it is disturbed and needs to find a new, secure resting place. Feline in so many ways, the genet seems to be at its busiest in the middle of the night—even when the moon is at its brightest. In many species, night vision is better developed than daytime vision; hearing is good, too.

Most civet and genet species spend the daytime asleep in a sheltered place. For the African civet this hideout may be a cave, tree hollow, abandoned burrow, or just a sheltered spot in dense undergrowth. The African palm civet chooses the fork of a tree or a tangle of vines where it curls up in a ball, perfectly camouflaged among vegetation. Genets look for caves or hollows between tree roots—even

abandoned termitaria (termite mounds) or an old eagle's nest hidden among rocks. Few of these animals use their claws to dig or burrow out a den, and most shelters are temporary. Only a female with young may establish a more permanent shelter, but even then she is quick to move on if she feels unsafe.

Within the species, some live almost entirely in trees, some live only on the ground, while others are at home in either environment. True civets are generally the most terrestrial and favor dense ground cover; they are neither adept climbers nor particularly fast movers. The palm civets are among the most arboreal of the species—even the heavy binturong spends most of its time in trees. The African palm civet has a coat pattern that merges perfectly with the bark of trees, and it is a superb climber. The common genet is at home in either environment, although it is an agile and active climber.

Morten Strange/NHPA

R. V. Nostrand/Frank Lane Picture Agency

The bulky binturong (above) *is a surprisingly adept climber, aided by sharp claws and a gripping tail.*

in SIGHT

HOME IN THE TREES

Among the most arboreal of all viverrids, the African palm civet shinnies up and down the smoothest of tree trunks with ease. Although its tail is not prehensile, like that of the binturong, it does use it to brace itself against a branch, while the naked soles of its feet give added grip. The third and fourth toes on the hind feet are partly fused, which helps to strengthen their grasp, and the entire body is well muscled. The African palm civet can run along a branch on its hind legs and may even leap between the branches. If it feels threatened for any reason, it will simply "drop" out of the tree, with tail and legs spread-eagled, to land on the ground several yards below, unharmed and ready to scamper back up the trunk of another tree.

Most of these animals are fastidious groomers. They lick themselves all over and clean their faces by wiping them with a forepaw that they have first moistened with their tongue. Genets and palm civets groom with both forepaws together and also sharpen their claws by scratching them down the rough bark of a tree trunk. They give a catlike stretch on waking, arching their back as they extend first their forelegs and then their hind legs.

POETRY IN MOTION
Although the African civet seems to be a slow, somewhat ungainly mover as it slinks around the undergrowth, it can accelerate dramatically if it has to. When pursued, it will gallop, dodging across the ground and bounding over obstacles 20 in (51 cm) high without breaking its stride. The genets look far more graceful in motion, and when they are climbing up and down trees, they seem almost to be gliding. Like palm civets, they will often descend a tree headfirst.

Many viverrids are vocal, making catlike screeches, meows, and hisses—even purring when contented. Palm civets and the common genet, however, both lack a cry of pain. The African palm civet is one of the loudest, and its owl-like hoot is one of the eerie sounds of the African rain forest night. It can be heard up to 0.6 miles (1 km) away—and may be answered in duet by a neighbor. ■

Palm civets are excellent climbers. Like most viverrids, their eyes give good distance judgment.

505

HABITATS

While civets and genets are most readily associated with forest areas, they are also able to exploit a wide range of habitats. The African civet is perhaps the least specialized of all. Across its range—throughout tropical Africa from Senegal to Somalia and south to Namibia and eastern South Africa—it is found in all but the most arid, exposed regions. Lowland valleys, marshy and montane forests, grassy savannas, reed beds, and vast plains of tall elephant grass are all home to the African civet. Its principal requirement is adequate cover; as long as this is provided—through dense thickets or rocky outcrops, for example—this civet will even be found in relatively open and dry countryside.

Equally, the civets of the genus *Viverra* have adapted to a wide variety of habitats across their Asian range—they are found from Nepal and India across to the Malay Peninsula, the Philippines, Borneo, and the Indonesian islands. Forest, brush, and grasslands are the most frequent habitats, all affording sufficient cover. The small Indian civet,

---

OTTER CIVETS CAN DIVE BELOW WATER IN FRESHWATER FOREST STREAMS, POWERED BY THEIR PARTIALLY WEBBED FEET

---

which is found eastward from Pakistan through Southeast Asia, is mainly an inhabitant of grassland or forests. Unusual among these viverrids, the Indian civet digs its own burrow for daytime resting.

HIGH AND LOW

The genets are primarily inhabitants of Africa, ranging virtually throughout the continent except for the Sahara. The common genet also extends into the Arabian Peninsula and Spain, where it may be found near the top of the highest mountains. It has, in the past, also been spotted in France, Belgium, and Germany. Between them, the genets appear to have exploited all wooded habitats; it is thought that they originated in rain forests but quickly dispersed to woodland, adapting to differing conditions—even comparative aridity—as they were encountered. Where numbers of species are known to coexist, they tend to be found in slightly different niches.

The linsangs are all animals of the forest. The African species are confined to the West African woodlands between Sierra Leone, Gabon, and the forests of Zaire as well as the island of Fernando Po, off the coast of West Africa. The other two linsangs are inhabitants of Asia, the spotted linsang

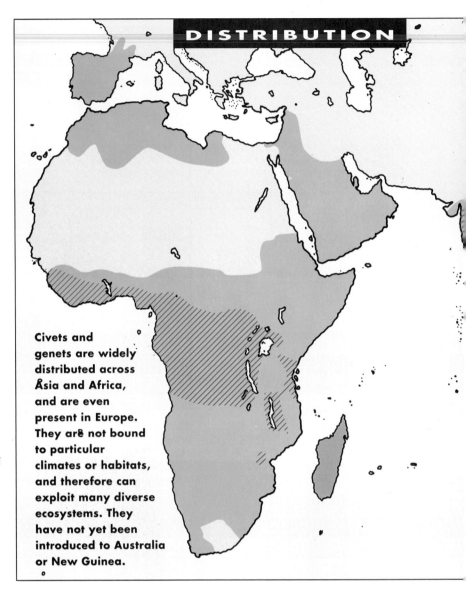

DISTRIBUTION

Civets and genets are widely distributed across Asia and Africa, and are even present in Europe. They are not bound to particular climates or habitats, and therefore can exploit many diverse ecosystems. They have not yet been introduced to Australia or New Guinea.

in SIGHT

COEXISTENCE AMONG GENETS

While the servaline genet is a true forest dweller, the common genet ranges more widely, even adapting to fairly dry habitats providing there is some ground cover. The large-spotted genet overlaps with both of these species, but is generally less able to do without water than the common genet and does not rely on heavily forested areas to the same extent as the servaline genet. In an area inhabited by both the common genet and the large-spotted genet, the former will generally keep to the higher, rocky, dry ground while the latter stays in the moister valleys. The forest genet seeks out habitats that are even denser and wetter than those preferred by the large-spotted species, while the giant genet is found only in the thick, dense rain forests of western Uganda and Zaire. The genet most adapted to arid conditions is probably the Abyssinian genet; its particularly pale, sandy-colored striped and spotted coat is ideal for the arid plains of Ethiopia and Somalia.

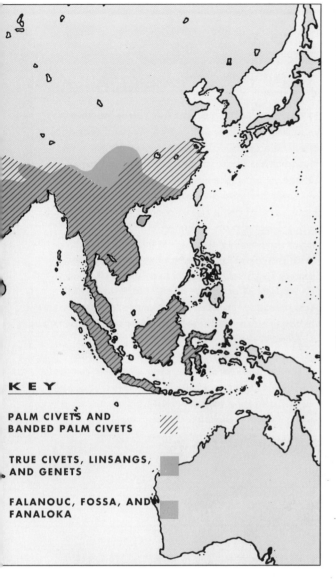

KEY

PALM CIVETS AND
BANDED PALM CIVETS

TRUE CIVETS, LINSANGS,
AND GENETS

FALANOUC, FOSSA, AND
FANALOKA

Francisco Marquez/Bruce Coleman Ltd.

A niche in weathered limestone provides a shelter for this genet (above). *It usually spends the day lying down, emerging at night or even a little earlier on cooler evenings.*

occupying the western areas, up to elevations of 6,400 ft (2,000 m) and the banded linsang extending east from Burma and Thailand into Malaysia, Borneo, and the Indonesian islands. The African linsang's preferred daytime resting spot is a nest of fresh vegetation that it builds itself. This it may share with others, and new nests are built every few days. At one time it was thought the nests were the abandoned nests of squirrels; now it is thought that, in fact, squirrels take over the nests when they have been vacated by linsangs.

HIGH-RISE CIVETS

Palm civets, too, are forest dwellers. All species, except for the African palm civet, are distributed through Asia from India, Nepal, and Sri Lanka eastward to the many Indonesian islands and Sulawesi (formerly Celebes). The masked palm civet has also been introduced to Japan. Living in isolation on small islands, viverrids have diverged subtly from each other over time. For example, the Kangean common palm civet, which is found on the Kangean Islands east of Java, may have thirty or more subspecies— some of which live in tiny forest ecosystems alongside unique subspecies of other mammals.

The African palm civet inhabits the rain forests of West and central Africa, and the forested savanna and gallery forests of East Africa. It appears particularly to favor areas with high rainfall and it spends most of its time at least 33–98 ft (10–30 m) up in the trees. This is actually quite a low level of the forest

Nick Gordon/Ardea

Perhaps the most versatile of all civets, the African civet thrives in forest or savanna.

507

canopy, where inhabitants are most vulnerable to larger predators. The African palm civet, however, is fairly large in comparison with the other nocturnal mammals that share its immediate environment. This, combined with its agility in the branches, makes it less vulnerable to predation.

The palm civets from the genus *Paradoxurus* are frequently found around human habitation, taking refuge in the roofs of buildings or in pipes. Although they may help to keep down the populations of rats and mice, they tend to make quite a racket at night, chattering away with noises that vary from soft murmurs to loud squeaks.

GROUND-LEVEL CIVETS

The banded palm and otter civets are mainly terrestrial, although all—even the highly aquatic otter civets—are adept climbers. Even so, they generally live in forested areas, often where the trees are very tall. These animals range across southeast Asia, from Burma and northern areas of the Indochinese peninsula through Borneo, Sumatra, and numerous small outlying islands.

The otter civets are nearly always found near streams or swampy areas. Interestingly, if chased, these animals tend to take refuge up a tree rather than in the water. Muscles that seal off the nose and

Joanna van Gruisen/Survival Anglia

FOCUS ON

CORBETT NATIONAL PARK

This area of some 317 sq miles (821 sq km) lies to the north of India, in the foothills of the Himalayas. In 1973, Corbett National Park became one of the first special tiger preserves when, with the backing of the World Wide Fund for Nature (WWF), Project Tiger was launched there. It was named after Major Jim Corbett, a hunter-naturalist who later became an author and photographer. Today, there is an inner core of the park—an area of some 124 sq miles (321 sq km)—where no human intrusion is allowed.

The park comprises a long valley through which the River Ramganga flows. Three parallel ridge systems run through the area, and each is densely forested. At other levels can be found savannas, with a rich variety of grasses. At the southwestern border there is a large reservoir created by Asia's largest earthen dam. At first this interfered with the migration routes of the park's elephants, but these animals soon established new paths.

The elephant is just one of many mammals to frequent the park—there are some fifty species in all, including leopards, jungle cats, Himalayan black bears, otters, porcupines, dholes, jackals, wild boars, and various antelopes together with a subspecies of the masked palm civet and the Indian gray mongoose.

TEMPERATURE AND RAINFALL

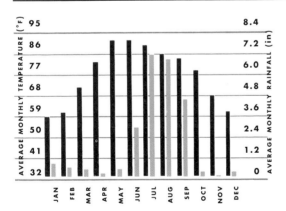

■ TEMPERATURE

RAINFALL

During the cold season (November–February) there are overnight frosts, but in the hot season (March–June) temperatures soar to 112°F (44°C) during the daytime. The monsoons that occur from July to October bring 60–112 in (1,524–2,844 mm) of rainfall.

ears enable them to submerge beneath the water surface, but they are neither particularly strong swimmers nor agile in the water.

The Madagascan species are all forest dwellers. The fossa is found from coastal lowlands up to elevations of 6,560 ft (2,000 m); the fanaloka mainly inhabits dense evergreen forests, although it is not a particularly good climber and is generally found around the ravines and valleys; and the falanouc lives in the humid, low-lying rain forest in eastern-central and northwestern parts of the island. ■

NEIGHBORS

Corbett National Park is perhaps best known for its Bengal tigers, which have more than doubled in number since 1973. However, it is also home to nearly 600 bird and 25 reptile species.

BENGAL TIGER

This beautiful cat is one of the most valued animals of Corbett Park. It is still critically endangered.

KING COBRA

Largest of all the venomous snakes, the king cobra is fortunately shy, and will slink off rather than attack.

Neighbor illustrations Sean Milne

Corbett National Park initially covered an area of just 99 sq miles (256 sq km)—less than a third of its current spread. Located in northern India between New Delhi and the western Nepalese border, it occupies prime tiger territory, but provides equally suitable habitat for palm civets.

CORBETT NATIONAL PARK

RED JUNGLE FOWL

This splendid bird is the ancestor of the farmyard hen. The cock alone has the fleshy red wattles.

INDIAN PYTHON

This snake can reputedly kill and eat a leopard. It locates its prey through smell and heat receptors.

BLACK VULTURE

One of the larger vultures, this carrion specialist has been seen on clear nights feasting on tiger kills.

GHARIAL

The gharial is a surprisingly harmless fish-eater. It has been saved from extinction by captive breeding.

PALLAS'S FISHING EAGLE

This majestic bird of prey catches fish by swooping to the water's surface and seizing them in its talons.

FOOD AND FEEDING

Although classed as carnivores, civets and genets have as omnivorous and varied a diet as any group of mammals in the animal kingdom. They all include vegetable matter in their diet, to varying degrees according to species. The linsangs, for example, have a dentition that is adapted mainly to a diet of animal matter, while the palm civets, such as the binturong, tend to feed mainly on fruit, since their small teeth and flattened molars are ideal for crushing vegetation to a pulp.

DIVERSE DIET
The true civets have a menu that is astonishing in its variety and has been described as being as omnivorous as that of the raccoon. It includes mammals—from small rodents up to animals the size of an antelope fawn—as well as birds, frogs, snakes, and other reptiles; insects of all types, from grasshoppers, beetles, and cockroaches to fly maggots and termites; crabs and snails; birds' and reptiles' eggs; carrion; plant matter, from grass and leaves to fruit, vegetables, and nuts—all are on the menu. An African civet may eat as much as 4.4 lb (2 kg) of food in one night, but can also go without food for a week or more at a time. It has a curious habit of rolling in strong or unusual-smelling food, such as

in SIGHT

A BALANCED DIET

Just like cats, these viverrids need to include some animal protein in their diet. This gives them the necessary amino acids to insure the constant rebuilding and replacing of cells in their bodies. They do not necessarily have to get the protein from small mammals, however; a diet of fruit and insects will insure healthy survival, and many of the species that subsist mainly on fruit will largely supplement this diet with insects.

Illustration Chris Shields/Wildlife Art Agency

carrion, before eating it. Genets also have a varied diet, eating whatever is seasonally available, although their shearing carnassial teeth indicate that they eat more animal than vegetable matter.

HUNTING TECHNIQUES
Although civets and genets are included in the same subfamily and therefore closely related, they hunt and kill their prey in different ways. Genets tend to hunt with stealth, in the manner of a cat, although they are considerably more clumsy and less effective—which is probably why their diet is so much more unspecialized. Nevertheless, in stalking their prey they are silent and stealthy, crouching low and gliding along the ground. Nearing a prey animal, a genet attacks in one of two ways. It may launch a series of swift bites, each time maintaining a partial hold with the teeth until it reaches the head. Alternatively, it seizes the victim in its forepaws and mouth and pulls it backward under its body before rolling to one side to hold the prey fast with its hind legs. The genet holds the prey fast with its claws while delivering the fatal bite.

The principal difference between these methods and those of the civets is that the civets do not use their paws in the attack. Neither does a civet stalk its prey; instead it forages along the ground, its head held low so that it can use its senses of smell and hearing to the full. Happening across a victim in the undergrowth, it grabs it quickly between its jaws. If the prey victim is something that may fight back, such as a snake, the civet tends to throw it down quickly at the same time as leaping upward with all four feet off the ground. In a flash, though, it is on the prey again, delivering another bite and shaking it, often so violently that its spine is broken.

EGG THIEF
A common genet laps up the contents of a bird's egg—a key source of protein (below).

Flashing its razor-sharp canines, a common genet protects its kill with a menacing growl (right).

The civet throws its prey to the ground before delivering a fatal bite to the head. It consumes its prey quickly, tearing off large mouthfuls and swallowing them down with very little chewing. Fruit is bolted down in the same way.

The large Indian civet is a fearsome predator and will often kill prey much larger than itself. This it does by delivering a series of bites to the hindquarters as it pursues the victim, until it weakens it sufficiently to deliver a killing bite to the head.

The palm civets are among the most frugivorous of all these viverrids and, through the night, they tend to gorge themselves in a series of short bursts of ten minutes or so followed by a rest of perhaps twice this time to allow

Jane Burton/Bruce Coleman Ltd.

for partial digestion. Cultivated fruits such as figs, mangos, bananas, papayas, and passion fruit are all favorites, and they are especially fond of pineapples. They also eat coffee beans, digesting the hull but excreting the kernel—much to the delight of local people, who apparently prefer the taste of "second-hand" coffee beans. Again, largely unspecialized in their feeding habits, they tend to forage at all levels in the forest, from low branches to the high canopy. They use their tail and dexterous hind feet to get a

ADEPT PREDATOR

A banded linsang (left) devours a frog. This agile Asian species also eats birds, lizards, and fruit.

firm grasp on a branch, thereby releasing their forepaws to gather fruit or strike out at birds and small mammals. When catching the latter, the palm civet holds them fast and kills them with a series of rapid bites before gulping them down whole. It does not indulge in the shaking and dropping technique of the true civet, which, in its arboreal home, would inevitably lose it its meal.

The banded palm civets are among the most insectivorous of these viverrids, and their rather elongated, almost trunklike snouts are an adaptation to rooting through the topsoil and leaf litter on the forest floor. Earthworms and other soil invertebrates make up 80 percent or so of the diet. The otter civets have adapted to exploit the wildlife of freshwater streams. ◼

511

TERRITORY

While all civets and genets occupy home ranges that they scent mark, not all are ferociously territorial. Scent marking is a way of advertising a presence so that confrontation can be avoided, for these animals are dedicated loners outside the breeding season. Scent marking also relays relevant information about each animal's sexual condition: this is very useful for breeding purposes.

The African palm civet is as territorial as any of these species in that it defends its territory to some extent. This may be because it lives in a higher density than most other viverrids discussed here—between five and eight individuals per 0.4 square miles (1 sq km) compared to one in the case of genets in the same area. Several palm civets may eat peaceably in the same tree if it bears a particularly heavy crop of fruit; fighting usually occurs only over access to females.

Within a home range, there will be one dominant male and a few females. The male may tolerate subordinate males in the territory providing they do not try to mate with the females. Challenges often occur, however, and furious fights may ensue in which one or another of the males is often sufficiently injured to fall out of the tree and possibly even die.

African palm civets possess scent glands with which they constantly mark the branches around their home range. There are glands between the toes of each foot, along the midline of the lower abdomen, in front of the genitalia, and possibly under the chin as well.

MARKING OUT A TERRITORY

True civets are particularly well-known for their scent-marking activities. Within their home range, they tend to slink along well-worn, habitually used paths and will stop to scent mark frequently—every 262–328 ft (80–100 m) or so. Because of their long hind legs, their rump is higher than the head and these marks are usually placed about 12–16 in (30–41 cm) off the ground; they are arranged in a line on trees, rocks, and shrubs. The thick, yellowish deposit quickly hardens and turns brown, and its odor remains pungent for several months. A pair of civets may each mark the same spot, building up

SCENT MARKING

One of the more popular methods of making a territorial statement involves backing up to a tree and daubing it with scent from the anal glands (below right).

SMEAR CAMPAIGN

Marking made easy: A genet leaves traces of scent as it clambers down from a tree crown (right). Such deposits are pungent and long lasting.

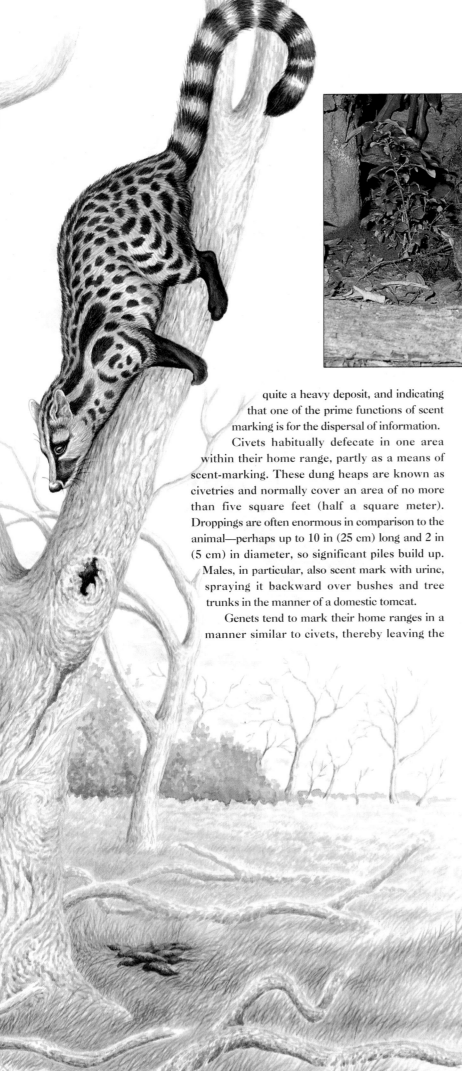

Nick Gordon/Ardea

quite a heavy deposit, and indicating that one of the prime functions of scent marking is for the dispersal of information.

Civets habitually defecate in one area within their home range, partly as a means of scent-marking. These dung heaps are known as civetries and normally cover an area of no more than five square feet (half a square meter). Droppings are often enormous in comparison to the animal—perhaps up to 10 in (25 cm) long and 2 in (5 cm) in diameter, so significant piles build up. Males, in particular, also scent mark with urine, spraying it backward over bushes and tree trunks in the manner of a domestic tomcat.

Genets tend to mark their home ranges in a manner similar to civets, thereby leaving the

The African civet often rubs its own familiar scent upon food before devouring it.

same kind of information about their sexual and social conditions. Males usually wander over a larger area than females and tend to roam at a rate of about 1.8 mph (2.9 km/h). Females seem to have a definite "homing" instinct; one female, released 21 miles (34 km) away from a home range, soon found her way back to the familiar territory.

ATTACK AND DEFENSE

When angry or frightened, genets exude a foul-smelling yellow secretion from the anal glands. But they do not spray this in the way a skunk does when under attack; only the masked palm civets are physically able to launch a spray through the air. Indeed, these species can spray over a considerable distance, and will try to aim for the eyes of the intruder in order to cause temporary blindness.

If a civet or genet does encounter another of the same species in its nightly wanderings, it generally reacts warily. If a confrontation occurs, each animal arches its back, erecting the dorsal crest and fluffing out the tail hair, which emphasizes the rings. Often it turns sideways to the opponent to accentuate the size of its body. It may "head dart"—lower and extend its head, waving it from side to side with the mouth open. This may be accompanied by hissing and spitting. The more submissive animal usually turns away or lies down.

A genet, in particular, lies down as a part of its defensive strategy, turning over on its back and defending itself with its sharp teeth and retractile claws. Genets and palm civets may use their retractile claws to hold an opponent in a fight, but they do not strike out and slash with their forepaws in the manner of a domestic cat. ∎

Illustration Robin Budden/Wildlife Art Agency

513

LIFE CYCLE

Many of these viverrids appear not to have a specific breeding season, although there are generally seasonal peaks according to location. In Africa, for example, births often coincide with the rainy season; African civets are capable of giving birth to three litters a year; genets regularly produce two litters annually.

Scent marking is clearly important during the mating season, for this is how a male will track down a female in estrus. Once a male and female have made contact, there is usually a fairly lengthy pre-mating period while they pace around one another and maybe rub faces. In both the African genet and civet, the male sniffs his mate's urine and then gives the "flehmen" response—in which he draws back his lips and wrinkles his nose, savoring the scent. The duration of the mating act varies; in the African civet it is rarely for as long as one minute, in the genets it is five minutes, and in the Madagascan fossa it is never less than one hour and often more than two.

The African civet generally gives birth to one to four young in a sheltered spot—such as an abandoned den, a termitarium, or a hollow tree. This is the only time when the female establishes a permanent shelter. The kittens are born fully furred, and their eyes open within a very short time of birth. By the end of the first week they can walk, they begin to play after two, and in the third week they will explore the outside world. At this stage, if one gets separated from its littermate, it gives a characteristic soft cough, whereupon its siblings immediately run to it, giving a similar call. The female calls as she returns from hunting, drawing the kittens to her.

GREETINGS

Solitary by nature, the male and female civet take some time to get used to each other (below) before mating.

Illustrations Peter Bull

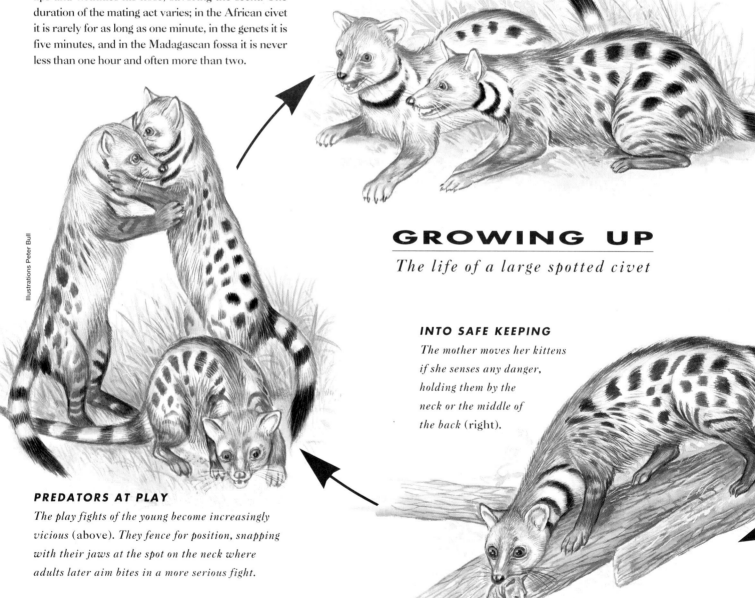

GROWING UP

The life of a large spotted civet

INTO SAFE KEEPING

The mother moves her kittens if she senses any danger, holding them by the neck or the middle of the back (right).

PREDATORS AT PLAY

The play fights of the young become increasingly vicious (above). They fence for position, snapping with their jaws at the spot on the neck where adults later aim bites in a more serious fight.

514

inSIGHT

TEAT-OWNERSHIP

Female viverrids, like cats, lie on their side to suckle their litter of tiny, hungry kittens. The genet sometimes wraps her bushy, furry tail around them to keep them warm.

Among the young of many viverrid species, a system of "teat-ownership" appears to develop naturally. This means that each sibling always suckles from the same teat. Even when tiny, some of these kittens have sharp claws, and if fighting occurred over a teat, they could inflict considerable damage on one another or on the mother. Since the claws of African civets are not so sharp, teat-ownership often does not occur until after the first few weeks. By this time the teeth have erupted, so again, fighting could have serious implications. Civet and genet kittens tend to "knead" the mother's abdomen just as kittens do—presumably to stimulate the flow of milk. They also tug at the teats like puppies. Genet kittens, in particular, purr like kittens as they feed.

Francisco Marquez/Bruce Coleman Ltd.

SECRET NURSERY

Although the kittens are well developed at birth, they are still vulnerable, and the mother is careful to nurse them in a safe spot well away from prying intruders (below).

Hollow trees and abandoned burrows make ideal nurseries for young genets (above).

short and their ears and eyes are shut tight. These do not open until, on average, the tenth day after birth. The female cares for her kittens assiduously, licking away their urine and feces like a cat or dog and defending them fiercely, even from their father, who is not above preying on his own young. The kittens begin to take solid food fed to them by the mother at six to eight weeks old, and although they begin to learn to hunt when they are three months old or so, they generally are not self-sufficient until they are twice this age.

The binturong is unusual in that the male helps with the care of the young. They are born after a gestation period of about ninety days, and although they are bigger than many of the young of other species, they are still blind and helpless at birth. ■

Weaning in this species may begin after one month, when the kittens begin to take solid food, but they will continue to suckle, sometimes for up to twenty weeks. When they start to eat solids, they may lick at the mother's mouth, apparently drinking her saliva. This does not encourage her to regurgitate food as in a dog, and it is not known for sure why they do it. Perhaps they gain enzymes or antibodies from the saliva, or possibly it is a response prompted by the smell of food recently eaten by the mother.

Genets give birth to the same number of young as the African civet, but they tend to be slightly less well developed at birth. Although they are furred, with indistinct markings already showing, the tail is

FROM BIRTH TO DEATH

AFRICAN CIVET	AFRICAN GENET
GESTATION: 60–72 DAYS	**GESTATION:** 56–77 DAYS
LITTER SIZE: 1–4, USUALLY 2–3	**LITTER SIZE:** 1–4, USUALLY 2–3
NO. OF LITTERS: UP TO 3	**NO. OF LITTERS:** 2
WEIGHT AT BIRTH: NOT KNOWN	**WEIGHT AT BIRTH:** 2–3 OZ
WEANING: UP TO 20 WEEKS	(57–85 G)
SEXUAL MATURITY: 1 YEAR	**WEANING:** UP TO 6 MONTHS
LONGEVITY: UP TO 28 YEARS IN	**SEXUAL MATURITY:** 2 YEARS
CAPTIVITY	**LONGEVITY:** 34 YEARS

PRIZED ODOR

CIVETS AND GENETS ARE HARD TO STUDY IN THE WILD, AND IN MANY
CASES THEIR STATUS IS NOT KNOWN. THEY HAVE, HOWEVER, SUFFERED
CENTURIES OF PERSECUTION IN THE NAME OF HUMAN COMMERCE

A s a group, civets and genets encompass a wide number of adaptations and characteristics. For carnivores, many have developed remarkably unspecialized feeding habits. To a great extent, this has allowed viverrids to colonize an extensive range, within which the different species occupy a wide variety of niches. Undoubtedly it has aided their survival over the centuries; it has also in many instances made study of some species in their natural environment—which is often dense, almost impenetrable jungle—particularly hard.

Bearing in mind that many of these animals have coats with exquisite markings, it is perhaps surprising that, by and large, it has not been the fur of civets and genets that has excited generations of humankind. Only a few have been hunted specifically for their fur—among them the small Indian civet and the common genet, the winter coat of the latter being prized in former times. Instead the feature for which humans have exploited various species since at least the 10th century has been the secretion from the anal glands—a secretion with a strong, musky odor known as civet.

VICTIMS OF INDUSTRY

Civet has most frequently been collected from the African civet, the small Indian civet, and species from the genus *Viverra*. The Malayan civet and the small Indian civet have been introduced to various other places because of this valued secretion—the Malayan civet to several islands of the East Indies, including Sulawesi, and the small Indian civet to numbers of islands including the Philippines and also Madagascar, where it is thought to be partly responsible for the decline of the falanouc.

The civet secretion has a buttery consistency. In its undiluted form, it has a somewhat nauseating, penetrating odor. When highly diluted, however, it becomes pleasant and it also contains fixative properties for other perfumes, particularly flower scents, enabling them to keep their smell for considerable lengths of time. This much has apparently been known since the time of King Solomon, for his perfumes were said to have come from Ethiopia, which has always flourished as the center of the civet industry. In fact, even since biblical times the perfume industry of the Middle East was supplied with civet from captive African civets. At one time civet was packed into the hollowed-out horns of cattle for exportation round the world.

FARMING THE CIVET

For centuries in Ethiopia and a few other locations, those civets valued for their secretion have been kept in captivity, often in extremely cruel, cramped

Nick Garbutt/Planet Earth Pictures

The Malagasy civet, or fanaloka (above), is steadily losing habitat on Madagascar, and is also hunted.

Nick Gordon/Survival Anglia

This map shows the former and current distributional range of the large-spotted genet.

///// **FORMER DISTRIBUTION**   ▨ **CURRENT DISTRIBUTION**

The Asian or large-spotted genet was once found in western India, in addition to being widespread throughout Southeast Asia. It has suffered persecution as a result of its chicken-thieving activities, and has also lost much of its habitat to agriculture and other commercial activity. It has not been seen in India since 1974, and may now be extinct on the subcontinent. Across the rest of its range, the large-spotted genet is being hunted heavily in China, and is reportedly becoming rare in Vietnam.

conditions in modern cages constructed from stout branches. This discourages them from roaming around an enclosure, depositing scent secretions as they go. Instead, many are kept in such a confined space that they are barely able to turn around. Once every nine to twelve days or so, their heads are restrained by a rope wrapped around the neck and held through the bars and the civet is then scraped out of their glands using a specially shaped wooden instrument, similar to a spoon or spatula. Such a collection might yield 0.4–0.5 oz (11–14 g) per animal.

In 1934, some 5,456 lb (2,477 kg) of civet was collected in Africa; at the time this would have fetched around $200,000. Most of this would have been used in the perfume industry, although when refined, the secretion may also be used for medicinal

A brace of spotted palm civets take refuge in the branches in Sierra Leone, West Africa.

517

purposes; it can reputedly reduce perspiration, help in the treatment of some skin disorders, and also act as an aphrodisiac. In India, some native people apparently also used the secretion to perfume or enhance the flavor of the tobacco they smoked.

Nowadays, the use of civet in the perfume industry has largely been replaced by the use of synthetic, chemically produced substances, but nevertheless there is still an extensive export trade of civet from East Africa and some Asian countries. There are probably 180 such civet farmers in Ethiopia today, with a total of around 2,700 captive animals. Each animal yields about 28 oz (793 g) a year, worth some $350. Between 1975 and 1978, Ethiopia exported about 5,300 tons of civet; most of this ended up in France for use in perfumes, despite the advances made in synthetic additives. These civets are not raised in captivity; instead the "farmers" go out and catch them in the wild as required. In one sense this is good for the animals, since there are few opportunities for large-scale expansion of the trade. This means, however, that the local farmer needs to monitor wild stock to be certain that they do not begin to deplete them.

DOMESTICATION

Although genets—the common genet in particular—are known to secrete a similar musky substance when marking their territories, they are

---

THE DOMESTIC CAT SOON SUCCEEDED THE GENET AS A MOUSER. NOT ONLY WAS IT LESS SMELLY, IT ALSO PREYED ON GENETS

---

not so widely kept as the civets for their secretions. However, they have apparently been domesticated and kept as pets from the time of ancient Egypt and of the Greek empire up to the Middle Ages. The Berbers, from North Africa, are said to still keep them. They have always adapted well to living near human settlements and they have long had a reputation for being good rat- and mouse-catchers, this being one of the main reasons for their domestication. However, they found themselves largely out of a job when the domestic cat became widely established in Europe and the Middle East. It seems that not only did it smell better, but it was also more efficient at keeping down rodents! In parts of Africa today, the common genet is considered a pest because it will raid poultry houses. In Europe, too, it is thought to have declined in some areas because of its attacks on poultry, and also game birds.

In Madagascar, where forest has been destroyed to a terrifying extent, all three subfamilies—the fossa, falanouc, and the fanaloka—are threatened to

RAIN FOREST DESTRUCTION IN SULAWESI

A. Greensmith/Ardea London

The island of Sulawesi, formerly known as Celebes, is the fourth largest island in the Republic of Indonesia. It straddles the equator, where the principal belt of remaining tropical rain forest lies. In effect, it comprises four long and narrow peninsulas that radiate out from a central area to the north, east, southeast, and south. The natural vegetation over almost the entire island, except for the highest altitudes, is rain forest—the natural home of the Sulawesian, or Celebes, palm civet—and like elsewhere in the world, it is gradually being destroyed.

Although the rain forest in Indonesia has not been cleared at an exhaustive rate—as in Africa, for example—it is, nevertheless, being systematically felled for logging and agricultural purposes. An estimated 7,720 sq miles (20,000 sq km) of forest is cut down annually, which

CONSERVATION MEASURES

● The isolated, moist rain forests in the Western Ghats in southwest India are home to the Malabar civet and brown palm civet. The latter is known to have at least two subspecies. Although these areas have been drastically altered by deforestation, logging has now been banned in order to preserve this vital habitat. There are also more than 20 protected areas in the local states of Kerala, Karnataka, and Tamil Nadu, several of which provide ideal habitat.

means that by the year 2000, Indonesia overall will have lost 10 percent of its resources.

The Sulawesian palm civet currently has the status of "Rare" on the IUCN classification, and at one stage it was thought to be almost extinct. However, current thinking is that, while it may exist in fragmented populations and is probably not abundant, it probably occurs over much of the islands where the rain forest remains undisturbed.

The problem of deforestation also affects the islands of Siberut, Sipora, and Pagi in the Mentawai archipelago, which are home to some unique and little-studied rain forest animals. Already more than 74,000 acres (some 30,000 hectares) of forest have been affected, and another 150,000 acres (60,000 hectares) have been assigned to a lumber company in Singapore.

CIVETS AND GENETS IN DANGER

THE CHART BELOW SHOWS HOW THE INTERNATIONAL UNION FOR THE CONSERVATION OF NATURE (IUCN), OR THE WORLD CONSERVATION UNION, CLASSIFIES THE STATUS OF CIVETS AND GENETS:

OTTER CIVET	ENDANGERED
SERVALINE GENET	ENDANGERED
FALANOUC	VULNERABLE
JERDON'S PALM CIVET	VULNERABLE
FANALOKA	VULNERABLE
SULAWESIAN PALM CIVET	RARE
OWSTON'S PALM CIVET	INDETERMINATE
HOSE'S PALM CIVET	INDETERMINATE
FOSSA	INSUFFICIENTLY KNOWN
ABYSSINIAN GENET	INSUFFICIENTLY KNOWN
JOHNSTON'S GENET	INSUFFICIENTLY KNOWN

Gerard Lacz/NHPA

THE PALM CIVET LIVES IN RAIN FORESTS, WHICH ARE THREATENED TODAY BY LOGGING ACTIVITIES.

● Indonesian national parks protect a number of viverrids. Hose's palm civet, for example, can be found in Gunung Kinabalu National Park in Sabah.

● Madagascar, which is home to the fossa, fanaloka, and falanouc, as well as eight endemic species of mongoose, has 2 national parks, 11 nature preserves, and 23 special preserves. They are, however, underfunded and poorly managed at present.

some degree. The fossa has been widely hunted and is particularly rare in areas near human habitation. In accordance with its IUCN status of "insufficiently known," it is probably the least endangered of the three. Indeed, it is held up as an example by the IUCN of how rare Madagascan mammals can be successfully preserved. This is one of the few animals, incidentally, to prey on Madagascar's unique species of lemurs. The falanouc and fanaloka have both declined through loss of habitat, the fanaloka now being confined to the eastern and northwestern rain forest areas only. The fanaloka is also trapped for its flesh. Recommendations have been made to provide it with legal protection, but the issue is complicated by the fact that the viverrid is, like many of its kind, a predator of domestic poultry. It has been suggested that, if protection were administered, villagers would nonetheless be permitted to trap and kill proven chicken-raiders.

Of the palm civets, subfamily Paradoxurinae, only the Sulawesian, or Celebes, civet and Jerdon's palm civet are listed in the IUCN classification. However, many of the others have been studied remarkably little and their status is unclear. As far back as the 1930s the small-toothed or three-striped palm civet was thought to be the rarest mammal on the island of Java, and there have been no confirmed sightings in the wild since the end of the 1970s. Even the quite widespread African palm civet has not been widely studied in its native habitat. There are even reports that palm civets on the Kangean Islands may be sharing their tiny habitats with undiscovered subspecies of the leopard.

David Keith Jones

Owston's palm civet can still be found in southern China, northern Vietnam, and northern Laos. It prefers to inhabit waterside habitats in both primary and secondary forest, but, like many viverrids, it is learning to cope with the ever-increasing proximity of humans. As a consequence, it is now under heavy hunting pressure.

The golden palm civet, native to Sri Lanka, is a highly adaptable species that has become accustomed to taking food—in the form of crops and fruit—from human settlements. Traditionally the former generations of villagers permitted the animal's raiding activities because it actually benefited them. The civet eats the fruits of the kital palm, which is valuable to the local economy as a source of palm wine. The kital seeds pass undigested through the civet and germinate, therefore propagating the kital. Sadly, the young members of the community think little of the civet's benefits and prefer to eat it. They bait it with palm wine, which the civet finds irresistible. In fact, some palm civets are referred to as "toddy cats" due to their fondness for alcohol—usually eaten in the form of fermented fallen fruit.

The banded palm civets of the subfamily Hemigalinae have two species listed in the IUCN classification. One of these, the otter civet, is thought to have been in Southeast Asia before the arrival of true otters, and may have been pushed back when these more developed animals arrived. Although it has quite a wide distribution, it is thought to be rare across its range. The banded palm civet, too, while not actually listed as endangered in any way, is another that is widespread but relatively rare across

Despite their rather smelly habits, genets have been kept as pets for centuries. Gifted with modest abilities as mousers and ratters, they are also playful.

its range, particularly in those areas where forest is being cleared. It has become an enemy of many local people through its tendency to raid poultry runs, so the villagers set traps for the civet made from rattan nooses.

Of the true civets, linsangs, and genets only three species of genet appear on the IUCN list. However, the large-spotted civet is said to be extremely rare in India; indeed, some authorities think it may already be extinct, while the more common large Indian civet is thought to be declining rapidly in Bangladesh. Some authorities think the range of the best known of all the species, the African civet, is becoming more fragmented.

Because of their secretive habits, little is known about the status of the linsangs, but it seems likely that where their habitat is under threat in India and parts of Southeast Asia, in particular, they are likely to be, too. The spotted linsang ranges from Nepal east to China and Laos. Probably the rarest viverrid in Thailand, it has not been seen there since the mid-1980s. It is thought to be more common in Vietnam, since it is turning up now and then in the local markets. It has only once been bred in captivity, back in 1986.

The aquatic genet is known only from a handful of specimens—only about thirty have ever been observed—so very little is known of its numbers. The common genet, on the other hand, is thought by some people to be extending its range in Europe, although it has been widely hunted because it preys on poultry and game birds.

Little is known about the Abyssinian genet, but it is certainly rare. There are suspicions that it may be affected by the desertification of Ethiopia and Somalia in the Horn of Africa. ∎

ALONGSIDE MAN

AN UNLIKELY PET

The shaggy, bearlike binturong is a shy, secretive creature of the night and an animal that rarely comes to the ground from its treetop habitat. During the day it is extremely slow and cautious if it is forced to move. Yet surprisingly, this is one species that makes a remarkably good and devoted pet. Not only is it said to be easy to domesticate; it will also become affectionate and has been known to follow its owner around like a dog. It is even playful, and provided that it has been raised from a youngster in a domesticated situation, it will retain its playfulness into adulthood. In a manner that seems completely uncharacteristic, it will run around displaying remarkable agility as it jumps into the air and flips over to land on its back. One kept as a pet regularly climbed up its master's arm for a game, using its prehensile tail in the ascent.

INTO THE FUTURE

With their fur in low demand and civet becoming less valuable as chemical substances and fixatives are used more widely, the direct persecution of civets and genets in the wild should be decreasing. However, as with so many animals, particularly those that favor woodland and forest areas, the chief threat to the survival of many species is the destruction of their habitat, "harvested" for its timber and cleared to make way for agriculture.

The IUCN has shortlisted the rarest species of viverrid, which include a number of mongooses. They list the four most threatened civets and genets as Lowe's otter civet, the Malabar civet, the falanouc, and Owston's palm civet. Based upon their research, they have drawn up a plan of action with five main objectives.

Their first intent is to gather as much information as possible about viverrids, since there is still

PREDICTION

HABITAT-DEPENDENT

Although some civets and genets show flexibility in adapting to different environments, many species are dependent upon moist tropical rain forest. If these forests go, then the viverrids will surely follow them in time.

much to be learned about these elusive nocturnal carnivores. They intend also to research, and demonstrate the feasibility of, the sustainable use of viverrids for human welfare. Civets and genets have brought widespread economic benefits in the past, and there may be some humane means of sustaining commercial exploitation. Their third, and perhaps most far-reaching goal, is to enhance public interest in the plight of viverrids by publishing the accumulated information. Captive breeding is another possible avenue; the fossa, for example, is now being bred in Duisberg, Basel, Montpellier, and San Diego zoos, and many other species are enjoying comparable success.

Their fifth and final point on the agenda is to enhance the survival prospects of viverrids by the protection and management of wildlife preserves, which are crucial to their long-term future. ■

CAPTIVE VIVERRIDS

The adaptability that has helped many civets and genets in the wild has meant that they have often proved relatively easy to keep in captivity. Many zoos around the world have kept various species of civet and genet, and many, too, have proved to make good pets. However, those in zoos are often perplexed by the keeper's cleanliness. The animals scent mark key points around their enclosures with secretions from the anal gland, which the keepers diligently clean away. This removes the animals' territorial marks. As soon as the deposit has been removed, they will mark again and again. Civets and genets kept in the same enclosure will deposit their scent marks on communal points.

The African palm civet is apparently easily tamed and has the added benefit of keeping houses clear of cockroaches, rats, and mice. Apparently, it becomes more lively around dusk, playing in a kittenlike manner with items such as balls of string, tugging with its jaws and paws. It will also chase after rolling objects, pouncing on them as if they were moving prey.

In captivity, the small Indian civet has responded actively to various experiments, apparently being able to differentiate between straight and curved lines and differing patterns. Experiments involved receiving food for making a particular choice, and, having once learned, the civet would return to the "correct" answer each time. It was apparently even able to pick out an elected pattern even if it was reproduced in a different color.

Illustration Carol Roberts

521

COYOTES

RELATIONS

The coyote, maned wolf, and bush dog belong to the dog family, Canidae, within the carnivore order, Carnivora. Other canids include:

GRAY WOLF

DINGO

GOLDEN JACKAL

RED FOX

BAT-EARED FOX

AFRICAN WILD DOG

DHOLE

Stephen Krasemann/NHPA

CLASSIFICATION

The coyote, maned wolf, and bush dog are in the mammal order Carnivora. There are two branches of the carnivore order: the dogs and the cats. One of the four families in the dog branch is the dog family Canidae, with 35 species. The coyote is in the genus Canis, as are the wolf, dingo, jackal, and domestic dog. The maned wolf and bush dog are in genera of their own.

ORDER

Carnivora
(carnivores)

FAMILY

Canidae
(dogs)

**THREE
GENERA**

**THREE
SPECIES**

Canis latrans
(coyote)

*Chrysocyon
brachyurus*
(maned wolf)

Speothus venaticus
(bush dog)

DOGS OF
MANY SIZES

FROM THE LEGGY ELEGANCE OF THE MANED WOLF TO THE SQUAT FEROCITY OF THE BUSH DOG, THE WILD DOGS OF THE AMERICAS ENCOMPASS THE EXTREMES OF CANINE EVOLUTION

The feature of countless images of the Wild West, the coyote is a legendary icon of the American wilderness. Yet of all the wild dogs it is the least well qualified for the role, for like its cousin the red fox it has learned to live alongside and exploit humans. In the face of persecution and loss of wild habitat, the coyote has flourished where other wild canids have all but died out. Today it is probably the most common large wild carnivore in North America.

In contrast, the wild dogs of South America are among the most obscure of all the carnivores. The elegant maned wolf has been little studied, and is now rare enough to be classified by the Brazilian government as endangered. The elusive bush dog has hardly been studied at all, and an estimate of its numbers cannot be made.

All these animals look very different. The coyote looks like a wolf, the maned wolf looks more like a long-legged fox, and the dumpy little bush dog

523

hardly resembles a dog at all—all of which has confused zoologists trying to classify these animals and sort out their ancestry.

The dog family Canidae contains some 35 species, ranging from the delicate little fennec fox to the big gray wolf. Most are lithe, leggy animals that run on their toes, with blunt, fixed claws that give good grip. The more lupine (wolflike) of the dogs can pursue prey rapidly over long distances, but lack the killing power of, say, the big cats. So wolves and many other large canids hunt in packs, to chase, bring down, and kill large animals that might otherwise escape a lone-hunting canid.

The smaller canids—the foxes—are less social, and opt for smaller prey that they can tackle alone. The vulpines (true foxes) are slender animals with pointed muzzles, large ears, and vertical pupils to their eyes. Like other dogs, they carry food to their young, but they never swallow it first and regurgitate on demand, as a wolf will. A fox always carries unchewed food in its mouth to give to its cubs.

WOLFLIKE IN MANY WAYS

These distinctions help to unravel the evolution and relationships of the New World wild dogs. In terms of anatomy, hunting tactics, social instincts, and infant care, the coyote is clearly a scaled-down wolf. Genetically, it is so similar to the gray wolf that the two species can interbreed and produce fertile young—a rare ability among animals.

Compared with the wolf, the coyote has a more lightweight frame, a narrower muzzle, and proportionately longer ears. It tends to take smaller prey, but pursues it with the same combination of tirelessness and cunning. It has the typically lupine build, with a deep chest for breathing efficiency and

The squat, secretive bush dog (above) *is the complete opposite of the statuesque maned wolf.*

T. Whittaker/FLPA

*Eyes fixed on the prey, a coyote pricks its sensitive
ears forward in anticipation of the chase* (left).

The maned wolf (above) *is a lone opportunist of
central South America's grasslands.*

stamina, and long legs for speed. The coyote can
reach a top speed of some 40 mph (65 km/h), and is
fully capable of chasing its quarry for 15 minutes or
more at a gallop.

HIGH-RISE HUNTERS

The South American maned wolf looks like a large,
leggy red fox; it was once even classified with the
foxes. Unlike true foxes, however, the maned wolf
has round eye pupils, and regurgitates food to its
young like a wolf. Yet unlike the wolf and coyote, it
is extremely unsociable, usually preferring to forage

RED COYOTES

**The red wolf of the southern United States
was once widespread from Florida to Texas,
but by 1970 only a small population in
Louisiana survived. A decade later it was
extinct in the wild, but enough captive
animals survived to enable breeding and
reintroduction into the wild in the late
1980s. Yet research has shown that,
genetically, red wolves are identical to
coyotes. It now seems that the red wolf is
actually no more than a hybrid between the
coyote and the gray wolf. If this is so, then
the breeders have saved a species that
never was: an animal that, in the north, is
regarded as a threat to the gray wolf itself.**

alone, and its carnassial teeth are relatively small. It probably started diverging from other canids some six million years ago. Relatives may have existed once, but they have left no trace in the fossil record.

Its long legs suit it to life on the South American grasslands, enabling the maned wolf to spot enemies and prey over the tall grasses. Its large, sensitive ears, too, are important to its hunting success. Like the coyote it is an opportunist, eating fruit as well as small prey, but it lacks the social instincts or the sheer muscle to bring down large prey. It is not too quick on its feet, despite its long legs, and is more of a stalk-and-pounce specialist.

SHORT AND SHARP

The elusive bush dog is squat and broad faced, with short legs, highly social instincts, and a carnivorous diet. Its low stature helps it slip beneath the stems of dense vegetation in its jungle home; it also swims well, and short legs may help here.

The bush dog's carnassial teeth are similar to those of the African wild dog and the Asian dhole; these three species may have a shared ancestry. The three are also the most dedicated pack hunters among the dogs, and the most social: Bush dogs sleep on top of one another, and hunt together. So although it may not look like a wild canid, the bush dog may well represent the ultimate development of the pack-hunting instinct that has made the wolf and the African wild dog the most efficient and feared of all the large predators. ∎

Color illustrations Kim Thompson

ⒶNCESTORS

HESPEROCYON

One of the earliest canids was the mongooselike *Hesperocyon* (hes-peh-ro-SY-on) of North America. It did not look at all like a coyote or even a wolf but bore distinctly canid features. For example, parts of its inner ear were encased in bone rather than gristle. On each side of the jaw, one upper premolar and one lower molar were modified into carnassial teeth, a feature of most carnivores.

MANED WOLF
Chrysocyon brachyurus
(KRY-so-sy-on brack-ee-UR-us)

Aptly but unscientifically described as "a fox on stilts," the timid, elusive maned wolf is the largest surviving South American wild canid. Its extremely long legs are probably an adaptation to life amid the long grasses of the South American plains, scrub forests, and marshlands, where habitat erosion and hunting have so reduced its numbers that it is now rare.

SOUTH AMERICAN FOXES

WOLF

TRUE FOXES

526

THE WILD DOGS' FAMILY TREE

The dog family Canidae (CAN-id-eye) can be divided into three main groups:
The true foxes (vulpines), the wolflike canids (lupines), and three species that
are difficult to place—the gray fox, bat-eared fox, and raccoon dog.
The lupines can be roughly grouped into three divisions: The wolf, coyote, dingo
and jackals of the genus Canis; the African wild dog, bush dog, and dhole; and
the maned wolf and South American foxes, or zorros.

COYOTE
<u>Canis latrans</u>
(CAN-iss LAT-ranz)

Essentially a smaller relative of the gray wolf but better equipped to exploit semiartificial habitats, the coyote has expanded its range as the wolf has declined. It is now common and widespread throughout much of North America, despite persecution from farmers and stockbreeders.

JACKALS

BUSH DOG
<u>Speothos venaticus</u>
(SPEE-o-thoss ven-AT-ick-us)

This short-legged South American species is a pack-hunting predator of dense forest. Extremely elusive and poorly studied, it is one of the most social of the canids and may be related to the equally social African wild dog.

AFRICAN WILD DOG

DOG BRANCH CARNIVORES

B/W illustrations Ruth Grewcock

ANATOMY:
THE MANED WOLF

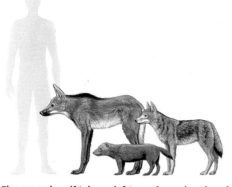

The maned wolf (above left) reaches a head-and-body length of some 41 in (105 cm) with an 18 in (45 cm) tail, and weighs, on average, 51 lb (23 kg). Males and females are the same size. The coyote (above right) has a head-and-body length of 27–38 in (70–97 cm), with a tail of 12–15 in (30–38 cm). The bush dog (above center) has a head-and-body length of 23–29 in (58–75 cm), with a tail 5–6 in (12.5–15 cm) long.

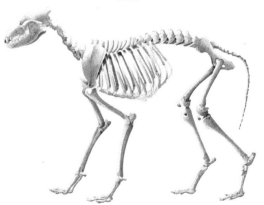

THE SOFT FUR

is always the same russet-red color, with a conspicuous black mane and black "stockings." There is no coat of woolly underfur, since the animal lives in hot climates and normally needs to lose heat rather than retain it.

THE FEET

are relatively broad, and the toes are capable of spreading to distribute the load more widely, enabling the maned wolf to travel over soft, marshy ground without sinking in.

THE TAIL

is moderately bushy, with long white hairs. It may not appear conspicuous, but this is due mainly to the length of the maned wolf's legs: The tail is a few inches longer than that of the coyote.

 X-RAY

MANED WOLF

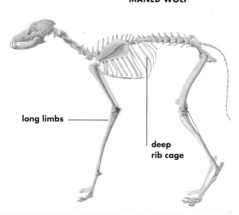

long limbs

deep rib cage

When looked at in skeleton, the maned wolf's legs seem immensely long even when compared to its rangy cousin the wolf. Visible also is the deep rib cage, which houses the capacious lungs. Although not particularly fast moving, the maned wolf needs plenty of strength and stamina to support its vertically extended frame.

WOLF

X-ray illustrations Elisabeth Smith

CLASSIFICATION

GENUS: *CANIS*

SPECIES: *LATRANS*

SIZE

HEAD-BODY LENGTH: 27–38 IN (70–97 CM)

TAIL LENGTH: 12–15 IN (30–38 CM)

WEIGHT/MALE: 18–44 LB (8–20 KG)

AVERAGE WEIGHT/FEMALE: 15–40 LB (7–18 KG)

GREATEST RECORDED WEIGHT: 75 LB (34 KG)

COLORATION

BUFF, BROWN, OR GRAY, WITH GRIZZLED LOOK
CREATED BY LONG, BLACK-TIPPED GUARD HAIRS.
CREAM OR GRAY UNDERFUR. BLACK STRIPE DOWN
MIDDLE OF BACK, AND BLACK TIP TO TAIL

FEATURES

LITHE, WOLFLIKE BUILD
LONG, SLIM LEGS
SLENDER, FOXLIKE MUZZLE
LARGE EARS

*The coyote (above left)
has a clearly wolflike
head profile, whereas the
bush dog (left) is closer in
appearance to a small
bear or a mongoose.*

BIG, MOBILE EARS

give acute hearing, essential for
locating prey amid long grass.

THE CHEST

*is deep, allowing the
lungs to draw in a lot
of air. In many canids,
such as the coyote,
this gives the stamina
necessary for pursuing
prey over long
distances, but the
maned wolf generally
uses stalking tactics.*

COYOTE

BUSH DOG

THE LEGS

*are extremely long,
probably as an
adaptation to living in
tall grass. The lower
leg bones are fused
together for strength
when running, as they
are in all canids, but
the maned wolf cannot
run particularly fast.*

SKULL

*The skull of the maned
wolf is more elongated
and tapered than that of
the gray wolf, but
otherwise there are few
differences. The maned
wolf's omnivorous diet
is reflected in its simple,
widely spaced molars,
while the long, narrow
canines are ideal for
seizing and holding its
small-mammal prey.*

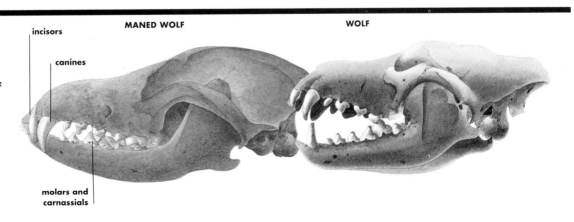

MANED WOLF   WOLF

incisors

canines

molars and
carnassials

HUNTERS AND HOWLERS

SOLITARY OR SOCIAL, HIGHLY ADAPTED OR SIMPLY ADAPTABLE, THE WILD DOGS ARE AMONG THE MOST EFFICIENT OF ALL THE AMERICAN PREDATORS

Ears cocked, attention focused, stepping silently and precisely, a maned wolf stalks toward a small cavy nibbling and rustling in the matted debris of last season's crop. Creeping as near as it dares, the predator freezes, poised on improbably long legs, then leaps—pouncing down with its forefeet to pin the luckless cavy to the ground. A quick snap, and it is gone. The maned wolf relaxes, licks its jowls, and trots away to find another meal.

THE LONE HUNTER

Solitary, silent, and wary, the maned wolf represents one extreme of canine behavior—the lone hunter. Probably the least socially inclined of all the wild dogs, it relies on its own resources to find food, outwit its enemies, and survive natural disasters.

> THE MANED WOLF WAS ONCE THOUGHT TO BE AN OVERGROWN FOX, PARTLY BECAUSE OF ITS DETERMINED INDEPENDENCE

Contacts with others of its kind are restricted to uneasy confrontations at territorial boundaries and the essential business of reproduction; outside the breeding season, even mated pairs have little to do with one another, although they share the same home range. In captivity a pair of maned wolves will fight if they are kept closely confined.

RUNNING WITH THE PACK

Wild dogs in general are social animals, and much of their behavior is shaped by the need to form and maintain social bonds and hierarchies. Many species have developed elaborate rituals for establishing rank without shedding blood, involving highly stylized postures and facial expressions. In many cases the subordinate animals in the group do not breed

and put all their energies into raising the young of a dominant pair. This is the situation with wolves, jackals, and, in some circumstances, coyotes.

The traditional image of the coyote is of a lonely nomad howling in the night, but although coyotes do forage alone, they are capable of hunting in packs. They may associate for this express purpose, because large prey is there for the taking, or they may form groups for other reasons and simply hunt together because it is convenient. Either way, association in packs has a radical influence on their behavior, affecting hunting tactics, choice of prey, territorial instincts, breeding arrangements, and, unfortunately, the increased likelihood of serious conflict with humans. A lone coyote may live almost unseen in a highly populated area, feeding

Dieter & Mary Plage/Survival Anglia

B. Gibbs/Natural Science Photos

A maned wolf yawns, revealing its typical canine teeth (above). *This canid normally hunts at night.*

A bush dog cools off at a forest stream (below). *A fine swimmer, it will even pursue aquatic prey.*

T. Whittaker/Frank Lane Picture Agency

Even in winter, the coyote manages to thrive on small fare such as rodents (left).

on vermin and scraps; a pack, on the other hand, is conspicuous, alarming, and capable of killing domestic animals—with inevitable reprisals from humans.

The coyote's ability to tailor its social arrangements to circumstances is one reason for its success in the modern world. Faced with a rapidly changing environment, an animal must be sufficiently flexible to exploit opportunities as they arise or it will be forced to take refuge in smaller and smaller areas of virgin habitat. As far as we can tell, this is the situation with the bush dog.

COMPULSIVELY SOCIAL

Despite the increasing presence of humans in its rain-forest habitat, the bush dog is still rarely seen and appears to retreat into the remaining forest cover at the first hint of human intrusion. Yet humans have seen enough of it to be certain that it is one of the most social of all the wild dogs, at the opposite extreme from the solitary maned wolf.

Bush dogs have been described as "compulsively social," with an insatiable appetite for each other's company, scent, and body warmth. A bush dog is probably incapable of functioning properly as a solitary individual, unlike a coyote, which operates in whatever mode best suits the situation, so social considerations affect every aspect of its behavior. Breeding appears to be triggered by purely social factors, and its highly carnivorous diet might be hard to maintain without the strength of numbers provided by the pack. ∎

531

HABITATS

Wild dogs were originally hunters of the plains. They evolved to exploit the climatic and vegetation changes of some five or six million years ago, when the forests began to give way to savanna and scrub and a new type of grazing animal began to flourish on the open grasslands. Quick on their feet, yet relatively poorly defended, these plains grazers—antelopes, gazelles, and wild horses—were there for the taking by predators capable of running them down. Accordingly, the big hunting dogs acquired the means to do so: long, slender legs with strong bones and stout claws, seemingly limitless stamina, and determination—ideal equipment for a prolonged chase over open country.

The coyote (right) *is one of the few large predators that enjoy a steadily increasing range. From the Great Plains, it spread to the north and east of North America during the last century, and now ranges from Costa Rica to Alaska.*

Dr. Robert Franz/Planet Earth Pictures

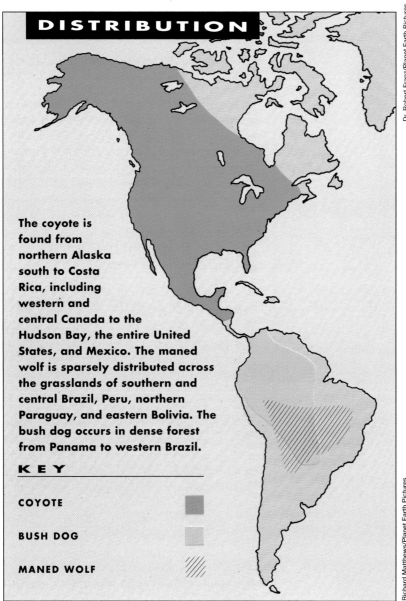

DISTRIBUTION

The coyote is found from northern Alaska south to Costa Rica, including western and central Canada to the Hudson Bay, the entire United States, and Mexico. The maned wolf is sparsely distributed across the grasslands of southern and central Brazil, Peru, northern Paraguay, and eastern Bolivia. The bush dog occurs in dense forest from Panama to western Brazil.

KEY

COYOTE

BUSH DOG

MANED WOLF

Richard Matthews/Planet Earth Pictures

Yet while it may have developed for speed on the plain, the canine body plan has proved infinitely adaptable, allowing the wild dogs to colonize a wide variety of habitats. Some species have kept their options open by retaining an unspecialized form, allowing them to move easily from one habitat to another; others have become tailored to specific environments. The New World wild dogs demonstrate both these principles.

SUCCESSOR TO THE WOLF

The coyote is a generalist. Common over a vast area of North America, it is found in a wide variety of habitats ranging from open grassy plains to mountain forests. As a high-speed hunter—one of the fastest—it is well equipped for preying on plains grazers such as the pronghorn antelope and mule deer, but it can thrive on farmland where mice and squirrels are the largest available prey and the staple fare may well be insects and worms. It also lives in suburban areas, combing through garbage dumps and household trash for tasty tidbits and even stealing the food left out for domestic dogs.

In the north of its range, in Canada and Alaska, the coyote is in competition with the gray wolf. Bigger and more powerful, wolves are capable of hunting much larger prey, so where such prey is available, they tend to go for the big game and leave the smaller fare. The wolf is just as adaptable as the coyote, however, and equally capable of living on scraps. So where prey is scarce, the coyote is often forced into prudent coexistence, having to make the best of smaller prey and carrion that have been ignored or abandoned by the wolf packs.

The maned wolf (left) *roams over South America's grassland, scrub, and swamp. A creature of the night and the twilight, it is rarely seen by day.*

K E Y   F A C T S

● The word *coyote* is derived from the Aztec name for the animal *coyotl*, which means "barking dog."

● Bush dogs have semiwebbed feet and may pursue their prey underwater like otters. A tame bush dog could retrieve stones from the bottom of a lake as easily as an ordinary pet dog retrieves a floating stick.

● Coyotes occasionally form hunting partnerships with American badgers. The coyote apparently uses its highly developed senses to locate burrowing rodents, then stands back while the badger digs them out with its powerful claws. The two animals then share the spoils.

● The maned wolf has the unique habit—for a dog—of digging with its teeth rather than its claws.

In the past, when the wolf was common throughout North America, its dominant position on the plains and in the forests drove the coyote into the marginal habitats, such as the mountain ranges and deserts. But the colonization of the American West radically altered the situation, as it virtually eliminated the wolf from the prairie states, leaving the field wide open for the coyote.

LONG AND SHORT LEGS

If the coyote is a generalist, both the maned wolf and the bush dog are specialists, each adapted to a quite different type of habitat. Having made their way to the plains of South America some two million years ago, via the newly formed land bridge of Panama, the ancestors of the maned wolf found themselves confronted with a sea of grass virtually devoid of big grazing animals. The grasses grow characteristically tall, presenting a problem to any animal that would hunt among them.

The maned wolf has solved the problem by rising above it. Its stiltlike legs probably evolved as a response to this particular type of habitat, enabling the maned wolf to see its way, locate prey, and keep watch for other maned wolves intruding on its territory. Yet although it is a grassland specialist, it also thrives in marshy areas such as swamp and river

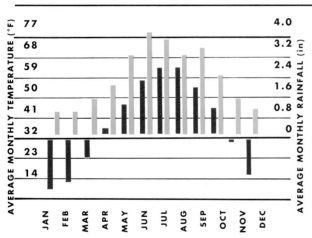

TEMPERATURE AND RAINFALL

■ TEMPERATURE
▨ RAINFALL

Rainfall is lower on Superior than on the other Great Lakes. The lakes absorb heat in summer, losing it again in winter: This gives rise, locally, to warmer winters and cooler summers.

margins, where its large feet help prevent it from sinking into the soft ground, and in scrub woodland and forest edge. Its range has been considerably reduced by the loss of habitat to agriculture.

The bush dog has specialized in precisely the opposite way, for rather than grow long legs to see over the tall grasslands, it has acquired very short legs that enable it to slip through the undergrowth of the South American jungles. This undergrowth is particularly dense at the forest edges and riverbanks, habitats that are especially favored by this semiaquatic hunter. ■

534

FOCUS ON

THE SHORES OF LAKE SUPERIOR

Gouged out of the landscape by glaciers during the last Ice Age, Lake Superior has a rocky coastline with steep cliffs and secluded bays, and the great evergreen forests of Canada come right down to the water. The lake is deep, cold, and relatively unpolluted, and, as a result, it is rich in wildlife of all kinds, both in its waters and along its shores, providing rich pickings for an enterprising predator and scavenger like the coyote.

For much of the year, many of the lakeside coyotes forage in packs for large prey or carrion. The lakeshores are frequented by moose and white-tailed deer, as well as gray wolves, lynxes, and bobcats. A group of coyotes stands a better chance of either killing such prey or gaining possession of a carcass and defending it against the other predators, although even a pack of coyotes is no match for wolves. The two species come into regular conflict, and wolves may kill coyotes in disputes over prey; consequently, coyotes tend to avoid areas where wolves are particularly active. Despite this, there is a good deal of interbreeding between the two. Their progeny, known as coywolves, are increasing all around the lake, although the hybrids seem reluctant to mate with each other.

Coyotes also prey on smaller lakeside animals, birds, eggs, dead fish, and insects, churned up after a storm. A coyote is not fussy about what it eats; that is a secret of its success.

NEIGHBORS

Of all the Great Lakes, Superior is the least spoiled by pollution. Freshwater fish and crustaceans attract flocks of birds, while mammals—and their predators—exploit the rich lakeside habitats.

GRAY WOLF

More powerful than the coyote, the wolf usually hunts larger game, such as moose and deer.

COMMON TERN

The wary common tern nests on small islands in lakes. It uses a spectacular plunge-diving technique for fishing.

Illustrations Edwina Goldstone/Wildlife Art Agency

LAKE SUPERIOR

Lake Superior is located on the southern fringes of the great conifer forests of Canada, and is the world's largest freshwater lake, with an area of 31,820 sq mi (82,414 sq km). The largest island on Lake Superior, Isle Royale, is now a national park, famous for studies on the interactions between wolves and their prey.

Hudson Bay

CANADA

Lake Superior

USA

Jeff Foott/Survival Anglia

| BEAVER | CANADA GOOSE | BOBCAT | COTTONTAIL RABBIT | MUSKRAT |

BEAVER
The beaver evades capture by coyotes by surrounding its lodge with a lake that it creates itself.

CANADA GOOSE
The Canada goose may nest in large colonies on the ground, making a tempting target for a hungry coyote.

BOBCAT
Spotted for camouflage, the bobcat lurks in ambush behind rocks and plants, waiting to pounce.

COTTONTAIL RABBIT
The eastern cottontail is a favorite prey of coyotes and all the other small predators around the lake.

MUSKRAT
The muskrat is an outsized species of vole and lives in a "lodge" home somewhat like that of the beaver.

HUNTING

Few carnivores are full-time killers, and this is particularly true of the wild dogs. The teeth of most species are adapted to process a variety of foods, including plant material, and anyone who has kept a domestic dog knows that there are few things it will reject as inedible.

DEDICATED PREDATOR

Of the New World wild dogs only one, the bush dog, has the reputation of preying regularly on animals larger than itself. It is no coincidence that the bush dog is also the most social: Teamwork offers the best chance of outwitting and overpowering large prey, such as the ostrichlike rhea, which weighs around 55 lb (25 kg), or the world's largest rodent, the capybara, which weighs

---

BUSH DOGS HABITUALLY HUNT IN PACKS OF EIGHT OR TEN, AND TO MAKE THIS WORTHWHILE THEY OFTEN GO FOR THE BIGGEST PREY AVAILABLE

---

around 100 lb (45 kg)—compared to the bush dog, which weighs 13 lb (6 kg), that is big. Teamwork allows the bush dog to exploit prey it could not otherwise manage.

Fleeting glimpses of wild hunting packs indicate that they often hunt by day, beginning at dawn with a ceremonial bout of calling. This has

Coyotes are far from fussy eaters. They will feast on prey, scavenge the remains of another's kill, or comb the rich pickings of urban garbage cans. This coyote is about to enjoy a tasty meal of trout washed up after a storm.

ZEFA

echoes of the wolf pack's prehunt chorus and probably serves the same function of establishing full communication and putting each pack member in the right frame of mind.

Communication is vitally important to a forest-hunting animal like the bush dog since pack members are often invisible to each other yet need to know each other's movements so they can select appropriate tactics to give

THE CHASE
is on. Running at the speed of a greyhound, the coyote is expert at catching jackrabbits.

in SIGHT

UNPACKING

Throughout the summer, when small game is abundant and easy to catch, most coyotes forage alone or in pairs. Where large prey of any kind is scarce, they use the same tactics in winter, but in some parts of their range, particularly in the north, coyotes switch to hunting and scavenging large grazing animals such as wapiti (elk), white-tailed deer, moose, and even bison. Such prey is a rich prize, dead or alive, and the coyotes will gang together to hunt as a pack, defend their spoils, and even drive other predators off their kills. But with the thaw, the pack may disperse again to concentrate on easier targets.

chase, outflank, or ambush. Bush dogs use a whole repertoire of calls, including whines, squeaks, whistles, and twitters.

NIGHT STALKER

At the other extreme, the maned wolf always hunts silently and alone, usually by night, pacing through the grass in search of rabbits, small rodents, armadillos, and ground-nesting birds, as well as virtually anything else edible. Its preferred technique is the slow stalk, culminating in a stiff-legged forefoot pounce that serves to nail the victim to the ground.

Maned wolves are also partial to fruit, and when fruit is plentiful, it may account for up to half their diet. Compared to most other plant material, fruit is highly nutritious and easily digested, so it is a useful food source

for a carnivore equipped with a relatively short gut adapted for processing meat.

ANYTHING GOES

The coyote is also an opportunist, ready to feed on anything from kitchen scraps to the carcass of a bison. Mammals account for some 90 percent of its diet, with most coyotes concentrating on small species such as ground squirrels, mice, and rabbits. It is an expert at catching jackrabbits, and 70 percent of the coyotes in Yellowstone Park bear the scars of encounters with porcupines. Coyotes will also eat frogs, lizards, and even fish, as well as large insects, worms, and carrion of all sorts. Wild and cultivated fruits are welcome in season, including blueberries, prickly pears, apples, peaches, and melons.

A coyote can forage for all these foods alone, using stalk-and-pounce tactics to secure small prey.

Illustration Robin Bouttell/Wildlife Art Agency

THE KILL

Pinned to the ground by a pouncing coyote and caught between its razor-sharp teeth, the jackrabbit has no hope of escape.

But in some situations, coyotes form hunting packs of four to six closely related adults. A big kill is worth working for, and the pack will chase a deer or antelope for up to 1,300 ft (396 m) at high speed, sometimes running in relays to spread the load. After the kill, each eats its fill and caches the surplus, for food is not always easy to come by—in the northern winters, for example, stored food may be their only security against starvation. ∎

PRONGHORN	MEADOW VOLE	FISH	MULE DEER	JACKRABBIT

Prey illustrations Ruth Grewcock

TERRITORY

Like many animals, the coyote stakes a claim to its home terrain and, to varying degrees, discourages neighboring coyotes from poaching on its patch. It is particularly possessive of the area immediately surrounding its breeding den and will defend this vigorously against intruders, but beyond this zone—known as the territory—it may be more tolerant. It often has to be, because the area it roams regularly—the home range—is generally too big to defend effectively without expending an unreasonable amount of energy.

So the coyote compromises. It does so simply by making sure that all the neighbors know exactly where it has been. By advertising its presence like this, it may deter trespassers; at the very least it keeps everyone informed and may prevent tense, possibly violent confrontations.

SCENT MARKING

The coyote claims its terrain by urinating on it. Like all dogs, coyotes are fascinated by the scent of each other's urine, because it provides them with so much information about the identity, sex, sexual condition, health, diet, and even age of the

Illustration Simon Turvey/Wildlife Art Agency

© John Shaw/Bruce Coleman Ltd.

individual. The same goes for another dog's scats (feces). Such scent marks are the equivalent of a canine grapevine, enabling all the dogs in the area to keep track of each other's movements, social context, and sexual state.

As it forages through its home range, each coyote investigates other scent marks assiduously to gather every scrap of information, then briskly marks over them. Whether this obliterates the original scents or merely adds to them—providing yet another layer of information—is uncertain.

Either way, it is obvious that the scent marks of other coyotes do not always act as barriers. They simply inform the discoverer that he or she has entered the home range of a neighbor or neighbors, and probably prevent further intrusion by eroding the trespasser's confidence. By contrast, a resident's confidence is reinforced by the familiar scents surrounding it, and if there is any confrontation, the animal with scent on its side will inevitably win.

The home ranges of coyotes may extend over

A lone coyote.

STAKING A CLAIM

STAKING A CLAIM *over territory involves the entire pack. Individual bush dogs spray trees, the ground—and each other— with urine.*

of areas that have been claimed by pairs, like vagrants camping on suburban roadsides.

LOOSE PARTNERSHIP

The territorial arrangements of the maned wolf are still something of a mystery, but it is thought that each pair may occupy an exclusive territory extending over some 12 square miles (30 square kilometers). During the breeding season the two may hunt together through this area, covering 20 miles (32 kilometers) or more each night in their search for food, but during the rest of the year they seem to ignore each other, despite sharing the same space.

Nomadic, unmated individuals behave like lone coyotes, carefully avoiding occupied territories and monitoring scent marks for clues that may lead them to vacant plots. Like coyotes, maned wolves use both urine and scats for scent marking; males seem to be more territorial.

FAMILIAR SMELL

The territoriality of bush dogs is even more mysterious. All we know is that they show great enthusiasm for scent marking as a pack, taking turns to spray the same object (and each other) with their urine. This probably serves to stake a territorial claim on the object, and may also help bond the pack together by impregnating them with the same smell. ■

3–30 square miles (8–80 square kilometers), depending on their social situation and food availability. Where home ranges are small, they can be defended as exclusive territories, and one coyote population studied in Colorado showed no overlap at all between the home ranges of resident pairs.

Unmated males tend to roam farther afield than females or pairs. In northern Minnesota, male home ranges were found to average 26 square miles (68 square kilometers), overlapping considerably at the boundaries, whereas female ranges averaged 6 square miles (16 square kilometers) with no overlap.

DEFENDING THE HOME

The largest territories and home ranges are occupied by packs, which are extended families consisting of a pair, their infant young, and their mature offspring from a previous season. When there are four to six adults to feed, plus infants to rear, the home range of the group may have to be extensive; it may also be much better defended than that of a pair relying on its own resources.

Conversely, the home range of a solitary coyote is often not defended. Some lone coyotes are reduced to scratching a living around the margins

KEY FACTS

● **Maned wolves have never been seen in groups of more than two adults, and even family groups of parents and young are extremely unusual.**

● **Occasionally several packs of coyotes will gather together to feed at particularly rich food sources such as large carrion, particularly in winter. The resulting throng of animals looks like one big pack, but there is little social organization and the aggregation soon breaks up when the food supply is exhausted.**

● **Female bush dogs are more socially competitive than the males, suggesting that they may fight for breeding rights like African wild dogs.**

● **A maned wolf may make its presence plain to an intruding neighbor by standing in profile on the skyline with its fur bristled up and back arched, warning the other individual to move away.**

● **Male maned wolves show more enthusiasm for territorial defense than the females of the species.**

SOCIAL STRUCTURE

The foundation of canine society is the mated pair. However complex the social arrangements of a species may become, a mated pair remains the basis of the group or pack. And however fluid the makeup of the pack may be, the pair remains constant. Even the maned wolf, least social of the canids, maintains a strong pair bond throughout the breeding period, and although the two may rarely acknowledge one another at other times, they share the same territory—a privilege denied to neighboring maned wolves—and renew their intimacy each successive breeding season.

Coyotes also form pairs that may stay together for life, occupying well-defined territories, but unlike maned wolves these "resident pairs" live and hunt together throughout the year.

A pair has a fairly straightforward relationship, but in some circumstances coyotes form packs, and things become more complicated. The basic structure is simple enough, however. A typical pack is

A LONE COYOTE IS USUALLY A NOMADIC ANIMAL WITHOUT A TERRITORY OF ITS OWN

not just an aggregation of like-minded individuals, like a street gang: It is essentially an extended family consisting of a mated pair and various offspring from previous years, plus the current season's pups.

DELAYED DISPERSAL

The reasons why coyote families stay together probably have to do with the interaction of coyote and prey densities. Usually the offspring of a resident pair disperse in their first year, traveling up to 100 miles (160 kilometers) before settling down. Some travel farther: One radio-tracked female covered 338 miles (544 kilometers) in a year. In some cases, however, some or all of the adolescents stay with their parents until after the birth of the next litter, or even longer, before setting out to find territories of their own—a phenomenon known as "delayed dispersal." Depending on the number of young in a litter, and how long they stay, such a family group may contain anything from four to ten adults and subadults: a force to be reckoned with.

Delayed dispersal seems to be most common in areas where the coyotes are protected and have access to large game, and rare in regions where the animals are persecuted and forced to live on vermin and scraps. Early travelers in North America

regarded coyotes as typically pack animals, like wolves; Lewis and Clark, who made a pioneering journey through the American West in 1804–1806, noted that coyotes generally lived in bands of 10–12 and were rarely seen alone. So it is possible that early dispersal, with coyotes living alone or in pairs, is an adaptation to human colonization of the landscape, with all its implications.

Out in the wilderness pack-living coyotes enjoy definite advantages, particularly in winter. In Grand Teton National Park, Wyoming, coyotes in packs seem better equipped to survive snowy winters, apparently because a pack has the collective muscle to claim and defend the carcasses of large grazing animals in the face of other scavengers. Packs also hunt cooperatively for large prey, such as deer, but in Wyoming, at any rate, this appears to be a secondary consideration.

TOP DOGS

There is a definite hierarchy within each pack. At the top of the heap are the alpha male and female: the mated pair. They have equal rank, and all the other coyotes defer to them. Below the alpha pair the status of each animal seems to be defined by its role in the breeding system. In any pack, only the alpha pair actually mate and produce pups, but to varying extents the other coyotes help to rear

A LONE COYOTE may be able to scratch a living on the margins of a pack's territory, but intruding on their kill will be overstepping the mark.

them. The most active of these "helpers" have the highest status in the pack beneath the dominant pair, but this is not the only reason why they do it.

Since all the coyotes in a pack are closely related to the alpha pair, any pups that they help to rear will share many of their genes. For any animal the main motive for breeding is to perpetuate its genes, so contributing to the survival of these brothers, sisters, and possibly cousins achieves the same end. For young animals that have not had a chance to breed themselves, this provides a valuable genetic insurance policy. Coyotes that have moved away from their parents' den and drawn a blank in their search

Ken Cole/Natural Science Photos

for mates may return and help with the new litter.

As each young animal leaves the pack to claim a territory and a mate of its own, younger siblings are often ready to take its place. So there is a constant turnover of subordinates, generally all offspring of the alpha pair. ■

A pair of coyotes in northern Montana. Whether or not they form part of a pack, the pair will live and hunt together throughout the year.

PACK HUNTING

can ensure richer pickings, such as an antelope. Any food left over will be stored for leaner times.

Illustration Robin Budden/Wildlife Art Agency

541

LIFE CYCLE

Female coyotes are capable of breeding toward the end of their first year, although many choose to stay within their parents' territory and delay starting families of their own. When a female finally makes the break, she may be courted by several eligible males during the winter mating season, but often only one will get the chance to mate with her. Once she has made her choice, the pair may stay together, living, hunting, and rearing their pups as a partnership for many years, sometimes for life.

COURTSHIP AND MATING

The courtship period begins in late December or early January, and the successful male gets his chance to mate during a two-month period from January to March. Mating can be a protracted business, since, as with most canids, the pair are locked together by a "copulatory tie": The male's penis swells inside the female and prevents withdrawal for anywhere up to twenty minutes.

The five to seven pups are born in spring. Blind and helpless, they are kept secure in a den, which may have been previously occupied by one or the other of the pair or acquired for the purpose.

The male leaves the nursery den shortly before the birth and moves into another den nearby, but he remains attentive, guarding the family and bringing food to his mate as she nurses the pups. From the age of about three weeks he brings food for the pups, too, carrying it in his stomach and regurgitating it in partly digested form like all lupine (wolflike) canids. If the mated pair are living as part of a pack,

THE NURSERY

burrow may sometimes be dug by the coyote. Alternatively, a disused den of another animal, a tree hollow, or a rock crevice may be used.

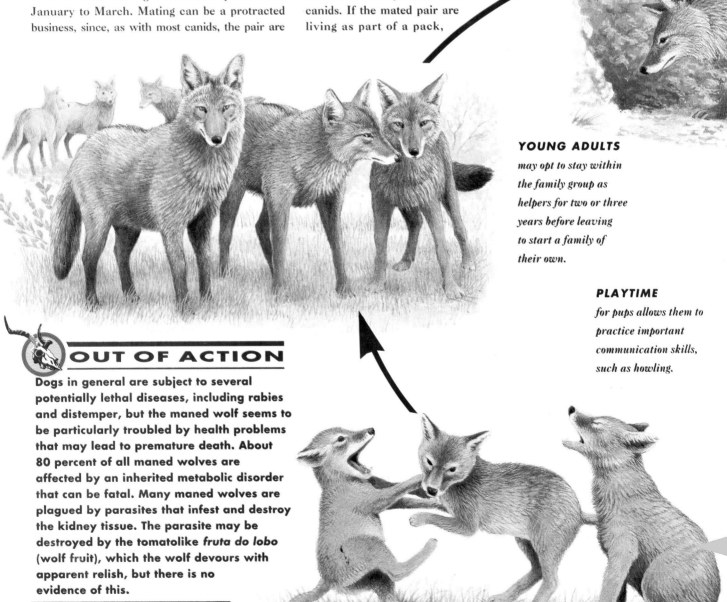

YOUNG ADULTS

may opt to stay within the family group as helpers for two or three years before leaving to start a family of their own.

PLAYTIME

for pups allows them to practice important communication skills, such as howling.

OUT OF ACTION

Dogs in general are subject to several potentially lethal diseases, including rabies and distemper, but the maned wolf seems to be particularly troubled by health problems that may lead to premature death. About 80 percent of all maned wolves are affected by an inherited metabolic disorder that can be fatal. Many maned wolves are plagued by parasites that infest and destroy the kidney tissue. The parasite may be destroyed by the tomatolike *fruta do lobo* (wolf fruit), which the wolf devours with apparent relish, but there is no evidence of this.

"helpers" of both sexes will also defend the den and bring food.

The young are nursed for five to seven weeks, and as they approach weaning age, they begin to play in front of the den. At eight weeks or so they start learning to hunt, but they are not fully grown until they are about nine months old. Around this time they may slip away to start completely

GROWING UP

The life of a young coyote

Young coyote pups venture to the mouth of the den (above), *all too eager to start play.*

independent lives, but many young coyotes stay for two or three years to act as helpers, or lurk on the margins of their parents' territory, reluctant to make a clean break.

LEAVING HOME

Leaving home can be a dangerous business. A lone animal may have to trek for 62 miles (100 kilometers) or more to find a vacant territory, risking attack from other coyotes, wolves, pumas, and armed hunters as it feels its way through unknown terrain.

Eventually, by careful analysis of scent marks, a young coyote may find an area that has not been claimed by others, or possibly a territory left vacant by the death of its owner. It may be able to move into an established pack as a very low-grade subordinate, or occasionally as a replacement mate for the sole survivor of a breeding pair. Otherwise it will have to fend for itself, and some coyotes entrench themselves in territories as lone residents. ∎

YOUNG PUPS

are fed partly digested food by either parent and by helpers. The food is often carried to the den in the stomach, and then regurgitated.

FROM BIRTH TO DEATH

COYOTE	MANED WOLF
GESTATION: APPROXIMATELY 63 DAYS	**GESTATION:** 65 DAYS
LITTER SIZE: 2–12, AVERAGE 6	**LITTER SIZE:** 2–4 (MAX MUM RECORDED 7)
BREEDING: MATING IN EARLY SPRING, BIRTHS IN EARLY SUMMER	**BREEDING:** MATING IN AUTUMN, BIRTHS IN WINTER–SPRING
WEIGHT AT BIRTH: 8.8 oz (250 G)	**WEIGHT AT BIRTH:** 12.3 oz (350 G)
EYES OPEN: AFTER 14 DAYS	**EYES OPEN:** 8–9 DAYS
WEANING: 5–7 WEEKS	**WEANING:** 15 WEEKS
INDEPENDENCE: 9 MONTHS	**INDEPENDENCE:** 1 YEAR
SEXUAL MATURITY: 12 MONTHS	**SEXUAL MATURITY:** 12 MONTHS
LONGEVITY: 14 YEARS OR MORE IN CAPTIVITY	**LONGEVITY:** 12–15 YEARS IN CAPTIVITY

Illustration Robin Budden/Wildlife Art Agency

Heather Angel/Biofotos

MIXED FORTUNES

DESPITE WIDESPREAD PERSECUTION, THE COYOTE HAS MANAGED TO SURVIVE ALONGSIDE HUMANS IN A CHANGED WORLD, BUT THE OTHER AMERICAN WILD DOGS HAVE NOT PROVED SO ADAPTABLE

Every year some 300,000 wild coyotes are killed for their fur. The details make grim reading: The animals are snared in steel-jawed gin traps, and are killed in such a way that their valuable pelts are not damaged. But as a large predator—and a wild dog—the coyote can expect scant sympathy from humans. All over the world big predators, and particularly wild dogs, have been persecuted for killing domestic livestock and scaring people.

Yet despite its unpopularity with humans, the coyote is not yet threatened. The activities of the fur trappers may be repellent, but they are restricted by game laws throughout Canada and the United States—indeed, the coyote is totally protected in 12 states—and while 300,000 is a lot of coyotes, the total population still seems to be large enough to

---

TO AVOID RUINING THE PELT WITH SHOT, A TRAPPER MAY KILL A COYOTE BY STAMPING REPEATEDLY ON ITS CHEST

---

sustain the loss. Up to a point, casualties actually create opportunities for other coyotes, enabling young animals to move into vacant territories and start families of their own.

North American farmers regularly complain about the losses inflicted by coyotes, and they may have a point; some sheep farmers are said to have lost up to 67 percent of their lambs and 20 percent of their sheep to coyotes in a single year. Coyotes are certainly capable of killing sheep, but there is some doubt whether these attacks are always the work of wild coyotes. Field studies suggest that the culprits are often feral dogs, which often roam in packs and menace livestock. On the other hand, sheep are not a wise investment, neither economically nor ecologically, in some parts of coyote range.

Wild coyotes seem to prefer wild prey where it is available. Studies of a coyote living on a farm in Indiana revealed that it preyed exclusively on rodents, rabbits, quail, and pheasants, despite the availability of domestic poultry. Coyotes are small enough to thrive on such game, and farming regions across the United States support healthy populations of coyotes that prey on vermin. But where such wild prey has been largely eradicated by pest-control programs, coyotes must turn to domestic animals, with dire consequences.

VANISHING WOLF OF THE PAMPAS

The prejudice that has caused the death of so many coyotes has also affected the maned wolf. Although primarily a predator upon small to medium-sized

The coyote prefers wild prey to livestock but is nonetheless persecuted by ranchers (right).

Oxford Scientific Films

A lone coyote surveys the snowbound landscape (above).

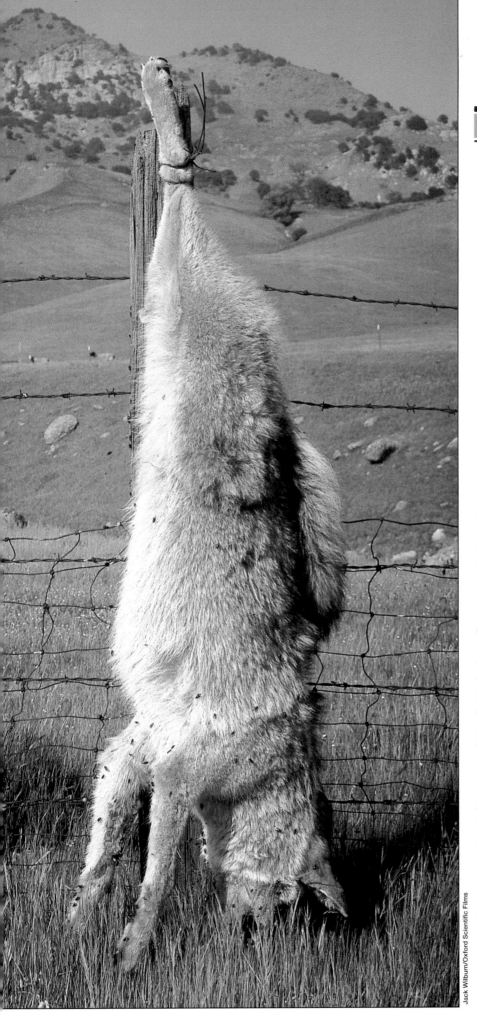

Jack Wilburn/Oxford Scientific Films

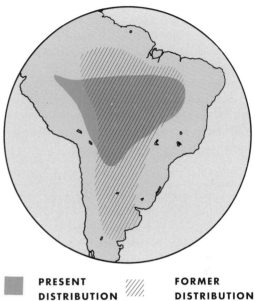

THEN & NOW

This map shows the former and present distribution of the maned wolf.

■ **PRESENT DISTRIBUTION**   ⫽ **FORMER DISTRIBUTION**

The maned wolf was once common from the pampas of Argentina in the south, right through to the far north of Brazil. Today, it is found in a greatly reduced range in central and southern Brazil, Paraguay, northern Argentina, eastern Bolivia, and southeastern Peru.

wild mammals, the maned wolf will occasionally take chickens, lambs, and other vulnerable live-stock; as a result, it is shot and trapped. But while direct persecution has taken its toll of maned wolf populations, the factor that has pushed it into the conservation statistics is habitat destruction.

In the late 19th century the maned wolf was widespread throughout the grasslands of eastern South America, as far south as the Rio Negro in Patagonia. But the 20th century has seen the con-version of much of the pampas—the temperate grasslands of Argentina, Uruguay, and southern Brazil—into cropland and grazing for cattle and sheep. The grazing lands are regularly burned off to encourage new growth, and in many places the native grasses have been partly replaced with exotic, high-protein species such as ryegrass. The insects that depended on the native grasses have dwindled; as a result, many of the larger animals that relied on the insects, and the ground cover yielded by the native plants, have also declined. The disappearance of much of their natural prey, combined with the

545

burning of their habitat and the increasing vigilance of armed farmers, has proved fatal to the local maned wolf populations, and the species is absent from most of its former range south of Paraguay.

Today it occurs chiefly on the tropical grasslands of the Chacos and the fringes of Amazonia, but even here it is scarce. Recent research suggests that it may be reduced to less than 2,000 individuals, which puts it on the same schedule as the tiger. But despite being the largest wild canid in South America, and considerably more picturesque than most, it attracts relatively little interest. Its habits are still poorly understood, and, at its current rate of decline, it may vanish forever before we discover the key to its effective conservation.

A DOG THAT'S HAD ITS DAY?

The maned wolf may be scarce and mysterious, but it is an open book compared to the bush dog. As an elusive denizen of dense forest and swamps, the latter is rarely seen and impossible to count. Its range appears to extend from Venezuela to Peru and Argentina but seems to be contracting with deforestation. Being a relatively small species, it may be able to survive unnoticed in small numbers, but as far as we know, it always lives in packs, hunting together for relatively large game—a habit that

DOGS IN DANGER

THE CHART BELOW SHOWS HOW THE INTERNATIONAL UNION FOR THE CONSERVATION OF NATURE (IUCN), OR THE WORLD CONSERVATION UNION, CLASSIFIES THE CONSERVATION STATUS OF THE NEW WORLD WILD DOGS:

MANED WOLF	VULNERABLE
BUSH DOG	VULNERABLE

VULNERABLE MEANS THAT THE SPECIES IS LIKELY TO DECLINE AND BECOME SERIOUSLY ENDANGERED IF NOTHING IS DONE TO IMPROVE ITS SITUATION. IN ADDITION, THE MANED WOLF IS CLASSIFIED AS ENDANGERED BY THE BRAZILIAN GOVERNMENT, SUGGESTING THAT IF NO ACTION IS TAKEN, THE SPECIES IS LIKELY TO BECOME EXTINCT IN BRAZIL IN THE NEAR FUTURE.

ZEFA

Most coyotes will steal livestock only if they cannot find any local wild prey, such as rodents.

would make it conspicuous and unwelcome in areas that have been settled for agriculture and stock raising. So it seems to be a poor candidate for survival in a world that is rapidly becoming overrun by people. Luckily there is plenty of wilderness left in Amazonia, but for how long? ■

ALONGSIDE MAN

EASY STREET

The highest densities of coyotes per square mile are to be found in the sprawling city of Los Angeles, where they have become adept at raiding the scraps and surplus of human society. There is plenty of space for the animals to den and breed, no farmers to trouble them, and a host of sympathetic residents. The coyotes probably do better in town than on the open prairies.

Urban coyotes were first noticed toward the end of the 1920s in the newer, more spacious districts of Canadian cities. The coyotes did little harm and a lot of good, destroying rats and other vermin and clearing rubbish. However, the coyotes have settled in to the extent that they are mixing genes with the locals. They breed with domestic and feral dogs to produce a race of so-called "coydogs," which seem to have inherited the worst traits of both parties and are generally far more of a nuisance than the coyotes themselves.

ZEFA

INTO THE FUTURE

The coyote is thriving. It has proved its ability to adapt to today's world, and although it is still persecuted, it may have weathered the worst; public opinion in North America is turning against fur trappers, and most city folk would rather feed a coyote than harass it. Legal protection in several areas has bolstered its rural populations, too.

The outlook for the other wild dogs of the New World is much bleaker. The maned wolf has been reduced to fragmented populations by persecution and habitat loss, and although it occurs within several wildlife preserves, such as the Serra da Canastra and Itatiaia National Parks in Brazil, its solitary lifestyle limits the number of pairs that can be kept comfortably within preserves. The species is protected by law in the wild in Brazil and Argentina, but the law is difficult to enforce; also, the habitats themselves are highly vulnerable to change.

PREDICTION

SAFEGUARDING HABITATS

For the maned wolf and bush dog, preservation of their wild, native habitat is the single most important advance in favor of their continuing existence. If the wilderness is lost, these dogs are not likely to survive in a changed environment.

The maned wolf's future will probably depend on the rate at which the remaining wild grasslands outside the preserves are exploited, and how. If such exploitation is limited to grazing cattle and sheep on the native grasses, the maned wolf seems to adapt quite well. It still has plenty of wild prey, and is unlikely to take lambs, chickens, or other livestock. But if the natural vegetation is replaced with exotic grasses or crops, the maned wolf often raids poultry runs—with fatal consequences. To date, maned wolf populations have dwindled and disappeared from areas that have been transformed into farmland, and this trend will probably continue.

The rate and scale of habitat erosion will also be crucial to the future of the bush dog. Our profound ignorance of its habits is a measure of its scarcity in areas inhabited and exploited by humans, and as such areas expand at the expense of the wilderness, so the range of the bush dog will contract. The species is unlikely, furthermore, to develop the ability to thrive in artificial landscapes. ∎

RELUCTANT CAPTIVES

The spectacular appearance of the maned wolf makes it a welcome zoo exhibit, but the species has not taken well to captivity. Unsociable by habit, it needs space to get away from others of its kind—and even its mate. It also needs space to stretch those long legs, for like most canids it is restless and wide-ranging by nature.

Maned wolves are bred regularly in captivity, but the pups have a poor survival rate. In several cases, young animals have been killed by their own parents, presumably because of overcrowding. Such events are particularly tragic because maned wolves have relatively small litters, and both parents normally invest a good deal of time and effort in raising the young.

Captive breeding is no substitute for the conservation of wild populations in their habitat. Nevertheless, if the problems of pup survival can be solved, it should be possible to sustain a captive-breeding program, if only to supply other zoos. *The International Studbook for the Maned Wolf* reported that 44 maned wolves were captured and taken to zoos throughout Brazil. For every individual that reaches a zoo enclosure, many are injured by and die in transit.

ACTION FOR CANIDS

The International Union for the Conservation of Nature (IUCN) has commissioned a series of "action plans" for conserving particular groups of animals, and one of these focuses on the wild dogs. The idea of the plan is to determine which species need conserving and how best to do it with the resources available.

The plan is, however, fraught with complications, since so little is known about the maned wolf and, in particular, the bush dog. Indeed, no one knows whether the bush dog is even rare. Any plan for managing the species would be based on so many broad assumptions that it might be worse than useless.

The longer we can leave large areas of the South American rain forest untouched, the better its wildlife will survive. This, however, is no excuse for ignorance. The more we can learn about wildlife in the remaining intact forest, the better future wildlife-management decisions will be.

Illustration Peter David Scott

DEER

RELATIONS

Deer belong to the Cervidae family, and musk deer belong to the family Moschidae, which is in the mammalian order Artiodactyla. Other members of the order include:

CAMELS

PIGS & PECCARIES

HIPPOPOTAMUSES

CATTLE

SHEEP

Ivor Edmonds/Planet Earth Pictures

Deer are two-toed ungulates (hooved mammals). They belong to the family Cervidae. This family is part of the superfamily Cervoidea, which also includes the family Giraffidae.

ORDER

Artiodactyla
(even-toed ungulates)

SUBORDER

Ruminantia
(cud chewers)

INFRAORDER

Pecora
(cattlelike animals)

SUPERFAMILY

Cervoidea
(deerlike animals)

FAMILY

Cervidae
(deer)

GENERA
seventeen

SPECIES
thirty-six

Moschidae
(musk deer)

GENUS
one

SPECIES
three

DENIZENS OF THE WOODS

A WHITE RUMP DISAPPEARING INTO THE DISTANCE IS ALL MANY PEOPLE SEE OF A DEER. THE PRIMARY DEFENSE THAT THESE SHY CREATURES HAVE AGAINST PREDATORS IS THEIR FLEETNESS OF FOOT

D eer are essentially woodland browsers, but species are also found on plains, mountains, and the arctic tundra. They are often confused with antelope.

Like antelope, deer have long, graceful bodies, short tails, slender legs, and long necks, and their large, round eyes are positioned on the sides of their angular heads. However, while antelope belong to the same family as cattle—the Bovidae (BO-vid-ay)—deer all belong to the Cervidae (SER-vid-ay).

There are 36 species of deer and some subspecies distributed throughout Europe, Asia, North Africa, and the Americas. Among the most primitive are the 3 species of musk deer, which were once classified in a separate family. Other primitive deer include the Chinese water deer, which is found in the swamps of China and Korea, the 5 species of muntjac, all of which are native to southern Asia, and the tufted deer of China and Burma.

Deer found in Europe include the roe deer, red

549

deer, and fallow deer. North American deer include the moose, caribou, roe deer, mule deer, and white-tailed deer, while South American species include pudu, huemuls, and brockets. The reindeer of northern Scandinavia and Greenland are considered to be a smaller, domesticated subspecies of caribou. Asian species include the rusa, hog deer, sambar, and sika. Fallow deer and rusa have also been introduced into Australasia.

The ancestors of modern deer can be traced back over 40 million years to a group of small four-toed herbivores known as *gelocids* (GEL-o-sids).

> DEER RANGE IN SIZE FROM SPECIES THAT WEIGH MORE THAN 1,765 LB (800 KG) TO THOSE OF NO MORE THAN 20 LB (9 KG)

These were followed by the *dremotheres* (drem-OTH-eer-ez), which were two-toed animals with teeth designed for browsing. Neither of these groups had antlers, but the canine teeth of dremotheres had developed into stout tusks.

True deer appeared first in Europe during the middle of the Miocene epoch, about 17 million years ago. One of the earliest was *Stepahnocemas* (step-ahn-os-EE-mas)—the ancestor of today's muntjacs. Muntjacs still have tusks, as do water deer and tufted deer.

Deer soon spread throughout the Northern Hemisphere, evolving a wide range of antler shapes and sizes, and there were some really spectacular

A mature male red deer (right) *lifts his head to display his magnificent pair of antlers.*

A male mule deer. Its antlers will attain full size by the time the deer is three or four years old.

Mark Hamblin/Oxford Scientific Films

Martyn Chillmaid/Oxford Scientific Films

A male Père David's deer (above), *its antlers in velvet. It will shed them shortly after this.*

forms. *Eucladoceros* (U-clad-os-er-us), which appeared about 5 million years ago, measured 8 feet (2.4 m) in length, and its antlers, each of which had a dozen points, had a span of 5.2 ft (1.6 m). Similar in body size, *Megaloceros* (MEG-al-os-er-us) appeared about a million years ago. It is often known as the giant Irish elk (moose), but it was

> IT IS THE MALE'S ANTLERS THAT
> DISTINGUISH DEER FROM ALL
> OTHER RUMINANTS. THEY ARE SHED
> AND REGROWN EACH YEAR

actually more closely related to the fallow deer than the elk, and was not confined to Ireland. Herds of *Megaloceros* roamed Europe during the period between the last ice ages. They finally became extinct about 2,500 years ago.

Antlers are made of bone, but they vary considerably in form, from the simple spikes of a pudu to the complicated, branched structures of red deer. Fallow deer and caribou also have branched antlers, but in their case the angles between some of the branches are filled in (a palmate antler). Only the Chinese water deer lacks antlers completely.

Deer are said to be sexually dimorphic—that is, males and females are quite different. Male deer grow antlers—most female deer do not. The only exception is the caribou, in which both sexes have antlers; the reason for this is probably that in this case the antlers have more than a sexual purpose.

Males grow a fresh set of antlers each year. It might seem strange that they should invest so much energy in their antlers, but the reason becomes immediately obvious during the rutting season. Rival males compete for females using the antlers in trials of strength; those that win go on to mate with the highest number of females.

Sometimes antlers become damaged. When this happens, a stag's chances of acquiring females become greatly reduced. If the antlers were not regrown each year, this situation would continue for the rest of the animal's life. As it is, the regrowth of antlers the following year ensures that a fit and healthy stag is not penalized because of accidental damage. ∎

ⒶNCESTORS
MEGALOCEROS

This huge deer scored high on points— that is, its antlers had many tines (points). Spanning 12 ft (3.7 m) and weighing 110 lb (50 kg), the antlers of *Megaloceros* (background below) were a seventh of the animal's total weight. Presumably, the more tines, the more impressive the stag and the greater chance of a harem.

THE DEER'S FAMILY TREE

The family tree shows the relationship between deer and other even-toed ungulates, such as the bovids (cattle), giraffe, pronghorn, and chevrotain. While all of these are contained in the order of even-toed ungulates—the Artiodactyla—they all belong to different families. Zoologists place the thirty-six species of deer in five separate subfamilies.

MOOSE
Alces alces
(*AL-sees AL-sees*)

In North America this deer is known as the moose. In Europe it is called the elk. A native of the Northern Hemisphere, it has now also been introduced to New Zealand.

All illustrations Simon Turvey/Wildlife Art Agency

MEGALOCEROS

EUCLADOCEROS

CHEVROTAIN

INDIAN MUNTJAC

Muntiacus muntjac (MUN-tee-a-cus MUNT-jack)

There are six species of muntjac, known also as barking deer because of the deep, barklike sound they make. They are found from India, Sri Lanka, and Nepal, through China and Tibet to Borneo and Indonesia and are small to medium-sized deer, with quite small antlers.

RED DEER

Cervus elaphus (SER-vus el-AF-us)

The red deer is the only one of the ten species in the genus to be found in Europe, Africa, and North America. The others occur in various parts of Asia. It is the largest of the Cervus species, although it will vary quite considerably in height and weight, according to location.

DEER

GIRAFFE

WATER DEER

Hydropotes inermis (hie-DROP-o-tees in-er-MISS)

The single species of water deer is found only in east-central China and Korea. Its scientific name means "unarmed water drinker." This deer lacks antlers altogether, but the upper canine teeth, particularly in the males, grow to form fairly long tusks that are slightly curved.

PRONGHORN

BOVIDS
(WATER BUFFALO)

ANATOMY:
THE RED DEER

THE ANTLERS
are used in trials of strength as stags fight to establish their place in the hierarchy during the rutting season.

A human being is dwarfed by the moose, the largest living deer, with a shoulder height of 55-92.5 in (140-235 cm). At the other end of the scale, a pudu is only about the size of a domestic dog.

3rd YEAR

4th YEAR

2nd YEAR

1st YEAR

Antlers grow progressively larger as a stag gets older. In its first year a red deer is known as a "knobber." In its second year it is a "pricket." In the sixth year, when there is a total of twelve points on the antlers, the head and antlers is known as "royal."

5th YEAR

6th YEAR

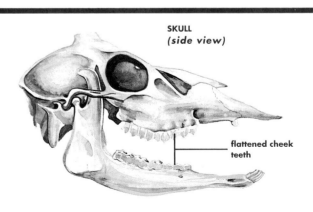

THE RUMP
often has a white patch, used for signaling danger to other deer.

THE CLOVEN HOOVES
are slightly concave underneath and help to provide a good grip when running.

Illustrations William Oliver/Wildlife Art Agency

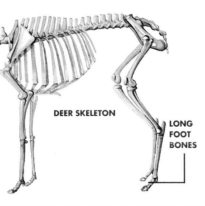

X-RAY

Deer have powerful legs for swift running and a long neck for grazing or browsing. Like all artiodactyls, a deer walks on the tips of its toes. And because these are on the ends of very long foot bones, the effective length of the leg is greatly increased, thus enabling the animal to run very swiftly.

DEER SKELETON

LONG FOOT BONES

SKULL (side view)

flattened cheek teeth

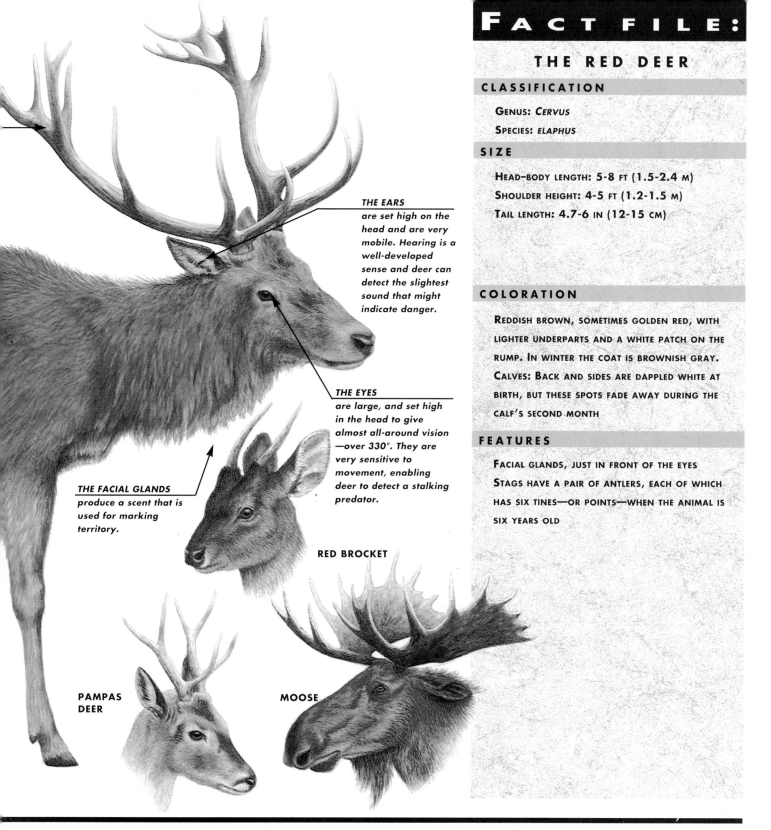

THE EARS
are set high on the head and are very mobile. Hearing is a well-developed sense and deer can detect the slightest sound that might indicate danger.

THE EYES
are large, and set high in the head to give almost all-around vision —over 330°. They are very sensitive to movement, enabling deer to detect a stalking predator.

THE FACIAL GLANDS
produce a scent that is used for marking territory.

RED BROCKET

PAMPAS DEER

MOOSE

CLASSIFICATION

GENUS: *CERVUS*
SPECIES: *ELAPHUS*

SIZE

HEAD–BODY LENGTH: 5-8 FT (1.5-2.4 M)
SHOULDER HEIGHT: 4-5 FT (1.2-1.5 M)
TAIL LENGTH: 4.7-6 IN (12-15 CM)

COLORATION

REDDISH BROWN, SOMETIMES GOLDEN RED, WITH LIGHTER UNDERPARTS AND A WHITE PATCH ON THE RUMP. IN WINTER THE COAT IS BROWNISH GRAY. CALVES: BACK AND SIDES ARE DAPPLED WHITE AT BIRTH, BUT THESE SPOTS FADE AWAY DURING THE CALF'S SECOND MONTH

FEATURES

FACIAL GLANDS, JUST IN FRONT OF THE EYES
STAGS HAVE A PAIR OF ANTLERS, EACH OF WHICH HAS SIX TINES—OR POINTS—WHEN THE ANIMAL IS SIX YEARS OLD

The upper jaw of a typical ruminant has no incisors— the lower incisors bite against a tough pad. Behind the incisors there is a gap, followed by the six premolars (three on each side) and six molars.

The premolars and molars are used for chewing tough plant food. Thus they are equipped with ridges suitable for grinding, rather than with pointed cusps.

Members of the cattle family have permanent horns. A horn consists of a horny sheath (made of keratin—the same material that forms nails and claws) inside which there is a core of bone. Once the velvet on a deer's antlers has been discarded, they consist only of bone; however, unlike horns they are shed each year.

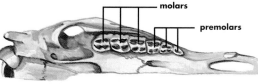

molars
premolars

UPPER JAW
(cutaway)

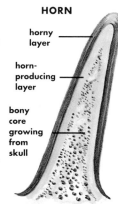

HORN

horny layer
horn-producing layer
bony core growing from skull

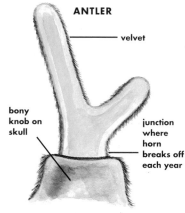

ANTLER

velvet
bony knob on skull
junction where horn breaks off each year

ROAMERS OF THE WILD

RUMINANTS ARE FASCINATING CREATURES BECAUSE THEIR HABITAT, FEEDING HABITS, AND MATING HABITS VARY ENORMOUSLY ACCORDING TO SPECIES

Deer, like antelope, may be found singly or in groups, and which lifestyle they adopt depends on such factors as size and choice of habitat.

Herbivorous animals that frequent open spaces often live in large herds, as this affords individuals some protection against predators, whereas in heavily wooded areas there is no safety in numbers, and in fact large groups attract too much attention. Smaller animals can be more secretive if they live alone. Thus deer such as the muntjac, Chinese water deer, Indian sambar, and brocket live solitary lives. Roe deer also generally live alone, but they can be found in small family groups—a buck with one to four does and their fawns. White-tailed

> VICTORIOUS RED STAGS RARELY STAY MASTER OF THE HAREM FOR MORE THAN A WEEK

deer form similar groups, and female red deer group together in fairly large groups.

Moose are solitary deer—a large animal such as this needs a huge amount of food and there is little merit in forming groups in which individuals would compete with one another for the food available in a small area. Only in the harshest winters do moose congregate together. They appear to help one another disperse the snow in order to reach the underlying vegetation. The area of trampled snow formed by such a group is known as a "yard." When the vegetation and brushwood are all used up, the group moves on to create another "yard."

FALLOW DEER

Fallow deer spend much of the year alone or in small groups. In the late winter and spring, however, they often form quite large groups. But even

Wapiti, or elk, rub their antlers against trees (above) *either as a show of aggression, or when in velvet.*

Rich Kirchner/NHPA

these cannot be described accurately as herds, since they are really just temporary aggregations of animals that have found a good feeding area; the basic family unit of the fallow deer is in fact just a mother and fawn.

CARIBOU HERDS

True herds are formed by caribou, which in summer range across the open tundra. Sometimes they may be found in small bands of between 5 and 100, but they also form herds of up to 3,000. In autumn they migrate back to the woods in the southern part

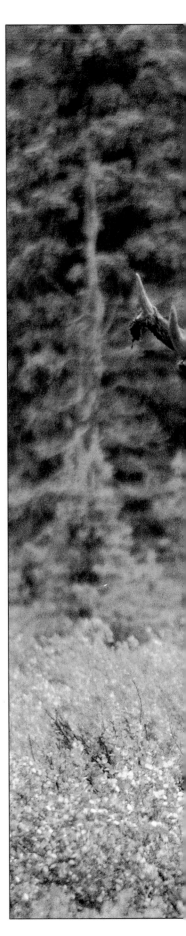

of their range, where they spend the winter. The caribou's large splayed feet are equipped with concave hooves, and patches of hair on the undersides help it walk across ice and snow.

Deer are built for speed: Running is usually the only way they can escape from danger. As in other ungulates, a deer's feet are greatly elongated, so that the heel bone is in effect halfway up the leg, and the animal runs on the tips of its toes. This enables it to run much faster than if the feet were

> RED DEER STAGS WITHOUT ANTLERS ARE MORE SUCCESSFUL AT FIGHTING THAN ANTLERED STAGS

placed flat on the ground. When running, many deer expand the white patches on their rumps in order to warn others of the danger.

Roe deer run in a series of leaps, which helps to reinforce the danger signal as well as allowing the fleeing animal clearer glimpses of the way ahead and of the danger behind. High speed can only be maintained over short distances, but this is often sufficient to escape predators. When hard pressed, caribou can gallop at 40 mph (65 km/h).

A bull moose feeding (left). *Bulls maximize their food intake before the mating season.*

A male roe deer in velvet. The protective velvet is lost when the new year's antlers have appeared.

557

HABITATS

Members of the deer family are found in Europe, Asia, North Africa, North America, and South America, and they have also been introduced into Australia, New Zealand, and New Guinea. They are typically woodland animals and many prefer to browse in dense forest. However, some species feed in more open areas, and deer can be found in almost all habitats, including arctic tundra, mountains, and grassland.

Caribou are found in the northern regions of North America and Siberia. During April and May they migrate northward into the open tundra. There they remain until June and July, when there is a movement southward to the forests. In

---

THE WAPITI, OR ELK, IS THOUGHT BY SOME PEOPLE TO BE A SUBSPECIES OF THE EUROPEAN RED DEER

September there is a second movement northward into the tundra for the rut, but this time the caribou do not travel as far as they did earlier in the year. After the rut the herds migrate southward again to their winter feeding grounds in the forests, although a few small groups remain in the tundra all winter.

The moose, the largest living deer, is also found in the far north. It inhabits the wooded areas of Alaska and Canada and parts of the Rocky

Most deer live in northern temperate climates. Fallow deer are native to the Mediterranean region; mule deer inhabit western Canada and the United States. Chinese water deer are found in reed beds and grasslands in China.

KEY

- MULE DEER
- RED DEER *(see also p.561)*
- MOOSE
- FALLOW DEER
- PERE DAVID'S DEER (reintroduced)
- CHINESE WATER DEER

Red deer (below) have increased dramatically in Scotland, and there is a danger of their damaging the forests.

William S. Paton/Planet Earth Pictures

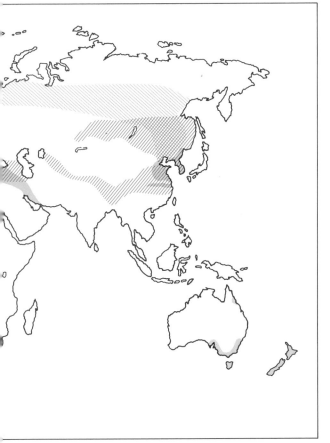

KEY FACTS

- Where there is adequate shelter, mule deer are relatively sedentary animals, but in more open landscapes they may climb to altitudes of over 6,562 ft (2,000 m) in search of cool pastures, returning to lower levels during the winter. These movements amount to a form of migration.

- Reindeer are the equivalent of cattle to the Lapps and other northern tribes, but it is a moot point as to whether the Lapps domesticated the deer or vice versa. Like caribou, reindeer follow traditional migration routes, the only difference being that people travel with them. They are used as pack animals, for drawing sleighs, and, of course, to provide meat and hides.

- Moose are excellent swimmers and will not hesitate to cross rivers or sea inlets.

Reindeer, or caribou, live in north Europe, Asia, and North America. Some races migrate to the Arctic in the summer.

Mountains in the northwest part of the United States. The species also lives in the Old World, where it is known as the elk. It can be found from Scandinavia eastward through Russia and Siberia to Mongolia and Manchuria in northern China. Moose are most at home in well-watered woods and forests consisting of willow and scrub with ponds, lakes, and swamps. During the summer, moose spend a great deal of their time wading through water, feeding on water plants. Wallowing in water has the added benefit of helping to keep off the hordes of flies and mosquitoes.

The red deer is considered to be a European species, although there are subspecies that live in

> IN SPITE OF THE MOOSE'S HUGE SIZE, ITS LARGE, BROAD HOOVES ALLOW IT TO WALK ACROSS BOGGY GROUND WITHOUT DIFFICULTY

various parts of Asia, North America, and North Africa. It inhabits mature forest by preference, but in Britain, where most of the forest has been cut down, red deer have been forced to become moorland grazers. Except for the period of the rut, the females, or hinds, live in herds separate from the stags, which roam singly or in small groups.

Roe deer prefer to live in dense cover, where they are small enough to creep about largely unseen. They are found throughout Europe, and in Britain this species was formerly very widespread. But as human settlements increased in the south, it appears to have been driven northward, and by the late 18th century there were no roe deer in England. Since then, however, they have been

David Middleton/NHPA

in SIGHT

LYME DISEASE

Lyme disease is a disease of humans caused by a spirally coiled type of bacterium known as a spirochete. The bacterium is spread by bites from deer ticks, which are often just as happy to take a meal of blood from a passing human as from a deer. The disease is dangerous and can cause permanent damage.

---

reintroduced into woodlands in many areas and today this is once again a common species of deer.

Fallow deer, noted for their spotted summer coats, are thought to have originated in the Mediterranean region, perhaps as far east as Iran and Iraq. Their original range has been considerably altered due to both extermination and introduction into new areas. They are common in parks throughout Europe and have been introduced into the United States. They are grazing animals and feed in open areas, but they prefer to shelter in woodland.

Related to both the fallow deer and the red deer is the sika of East Asia. This species lives in deciduous and mixed forests and has been introduced into many areas of Europe.

Similar in coloring to fallow deer are the beautiful and very common axis deer, or chital, of India, and the hog deer of India, which is found in herds in a variety of habitats, from lowland plains to the lower hills, among bushes, trees, or in bamboo thickets. Hog deer live generally alone or in small parties on grassy plains.

FOCUS ON

NEW ENGLAND

New England is a group of six states—Connecticut, Maine, Massachusetts, New Hampshire, Rhode Island, and Vermont—in the northeastern United States. This picturesque and historic region contains rocky coasts, sprawling mixed forests, and low ranges—the northern parts of the Appalachian Mountains.

Summers are warm, with temperatures occasionally soaring to 105°F (40°C), but in winter and sometimes spring, severe cold spells send temperatures plummeting far below the freezing point. Heavy snowfalls give plenty of opportunities for winter sports.

New England is probably best known for its warm autumns, when the foliage of deciduous trees, including ash, beech, birch, maple, and oak, produces spectacular displays of color.

The deer that thrive in such a colorful terrain include the moose, the white-tailed deer, and the wapiti, or elk.

TEMPERATURE AND RAINFALL

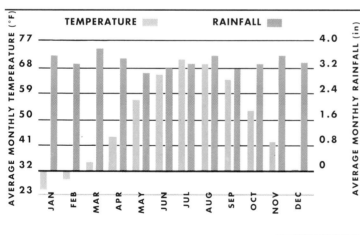

New England temperatures (represented here by Boston's statistics) peak at around 72°F (22°C) in July, and drop to 25°F (-4°C) in January. Rainfall is at its heaviest in March at 3.5 in (90 mm), but drops only to 3 in (76 mm) in May.

NEIGHBORS

The North American and Canadian terrain is rich and varied, comprising mountains, lakes, and forest. Deer share it with a wide variety of mammals, birds, fish, and insects.

SKUNK

Skunks are renowned for their unique defensive system—a vile-smelling, poison-gas–like spray.

DRAGONFLY

Dragonflies can travel at speeds of up to 60 mph (96 km/h), making them one of the fastest flying insects.

Illustrations Evi Antoniou

NEW ENGLAND RED DEER

The North American form of red deer is the wapiti, or elk. For much of the year the female and young live in herds, while the males form smaller, more loosely knit groups. The wapiti range extends east to west and north to south from Canada to Mexico.

NEW ENGLAND

ENEMIES

COYOTES
The wolf's cousin has increased in range in North America, because it is cunning and adaptable.

BOBCAT
Lynx rufus preys on small deer and rodents.

BEARS
Heavily built and strong, bears have few enemies. The grizzly is reputed to be the most ferocious.

EXTREMELY DANGEROUS

MODERATELY DANGEROUS

MODERATELY DANGEROUS

RACCOON

The raccoon family, Procyonidae, contains 16 species and is found naturally only in the Americas.

CARDINAL

This striking bird is found from the Colorado River through southern Arizona to California and Mexico.

GRASSHOPPER

Grasshoppers have special organs for receiving sound waves.

NORTH AMERICAN RED FOX

The red fox—Vulpes vulpes—is found throughout the Northern Hemisphere and is much valued for its fur.

ROBIN

The best known of all American birds, it is found in any wooded habitat, including parks and lawns.

FOOD AND FEEDING

Deer are essentially browsing animals—that is, they feed on the leaves of trees. However, although their ancestors probably survived entirely on this diet, today's deer tend to have more varied tastes. Different species specialize in eating different kinds of food, and diet may change according to the conditions and time of year. In summer, food is plentiful, but in winter it is often scarce and deer have to forage what they can while surviving largely on fat stored up during the summer. Some species travel long distances in search of food.

Roe deer are typical of the family. In summer

Deer are ruminant herbivores; that is, they feed on plant material, and digestion is aided by the presence of bacteria in a part of the stomach known as the rumen, together with the process known as chewing the cud.

Most vegetable matter is not nutrient dense and thus herbivorous animals need to eat large amounts. Like other ruminants, deer have no upper incisors; instead the lower incisors bite onto a hard pad in order to cut off the food, which is chewed using broad, flat-crowned premolars and molars. The food is chewed not once, but twice, while the bacteria are used to break down the cellulose of the plant cell walls.

Male wapiti, or elk, in winter, Yellowstone National Park.

SELECTING FOOD
Males select and defend the best feeding areas they can in order to attract does to mate with them.

in SIGHT

DEER DIGESTION
When a ruminant swallows partly chewed food for the first time, it enters a large part of the stomach known as the rumen. Here, bacteria begin to ferment the food, breaking down its tough, cellulose cell walls. It then passes to a second chamber—the reticulum—from where it is regurgitated in lumps to be chewed again. The pulped food is then swallowed again and passed to a third chamber—the omasum—where it is churned about and then passed on to the true stomach, or abomasum, where the normal mammalian digestion begins.

they feed on a range of foods, including grass, the leaves of broad-leaved and evergreen trees and shrubs, heather, and bramble. They are particularly fond of the young shoots of trees and can cause considerable damage in new plantations. In the autumn they eat berries and fungi.

Fallow deer have a similar diet. Grass is their main food, but if this is scarce, they will raid crops and also eat mosses, herbs, and the leaves of trees and bushes. In autumn they eat hard fruits such as acorns, beech mast, and chestnuts, and sometimes strip the bark from young trees, often killing the trees in the process.

In summer in the far north, caribou browse and graze on a variety of plants, such as birch, willow, horsetails, grasses, and sedges. In winter they eat the lichen known as reindeer moss and dried grass, which they find by scraping away the snow. They also chew cast antlers, which presumably helps to replenish the body's supply of calcium, ready for the growing of new antlers in the spring.

In the northern forests moose feed mostly on water plants during the summer. In winter they browse on the shoots, leaves, and branches of saplings, using their great height to reach high above the ground. Sometimes a moose will even bend a sapling to the ground by straddling it. ∎

Bud Smithey/Planet Earth Pictures

Bull moose have a varied diet and browse in trees as well as grazing grass.

KEY FACTS

Deer are normally shy animals that shun the company of other creatures. But the chital of India seem to have formed a kind of association with langur monkeys and will actively seek them out. The reason for this is that chital have learned that these monkeys provide an excellent source of food. The langurs feed in trees, but they prefer the leaf stalks to the blades, which they strip off and discard. These then provide a feast for the deer waiting below. A troupe of langurs drops about twelve tons of foliage each year, of which over half is suitable food for chital.

The association is not entirely one-sided. Chital have a good sense of smell, while langurs have more acute vision. This, together with the fact that chital and langurs appear to respond to each other's alarm calls, gives them a better chance of getting early warning of nearby predators.

FOOD

Deer are ruminants (they chew the cud), and generally feed on grass, shoots, twigs, leaves, flowers, and fruit of herbs, shrubs, and trees.

DAISIES	MOSSES	BLACKBERRIES	OLD ANTLERS

All illustrations Joanne Cowne

LIFE CYCLE

Mating in deer occurs during what is known as the rut—the period during which females come into heat and are served by the males. In most cases males compete for the females, but the extent to which they do this varies between species.

In caribou, for example, the rut takes place during late October and early November and the bulls serve the cows indiscriminately, without forming harems. Only if two bulls meet by chance is there aggression, and even then any sparring is very brief.

A roe deer buck generally mates with just one doe, whom he appears to court. In July or August he marks out an area by fraying young trees and scraping the ground with his antlers, sometimes marking the scrapes with scent from glands on his forehead. He then chases the doe, weaving a figure-eight pattern on the ground. Although the doe appears to be driven by the buck, the chase is followed by mating.

Among moose the breeding season, which

Although bull caribou rarely fight with each other, they do display to their prospective mates by thrashing the undergrowth with a side-to-side movement of the antlers.

The young of caribou are born in early June, while the herds are on their spring migration. Most of the calves are born within a fortnight of one another, which has several advantages. If they are born too early, they cannot survive the harsh weather and if they are born too late, they will not be strong enough to survive the following winter. And if all the cows have calves, the herd travels more slowly and there is less danger of some being left behind and falling prey to wolves and bears.

BEFORE GIVING BIRTH, *the doe may chase off young left from the previous year.*

YOUNG DEER *are especially vulnerable to predators, such as this golden eagle.*

Manfred Daneger/NHPA

CARIBOU MATING *Females give birth in spring in areas that will provide rich summer pasture.*

GROWING UP

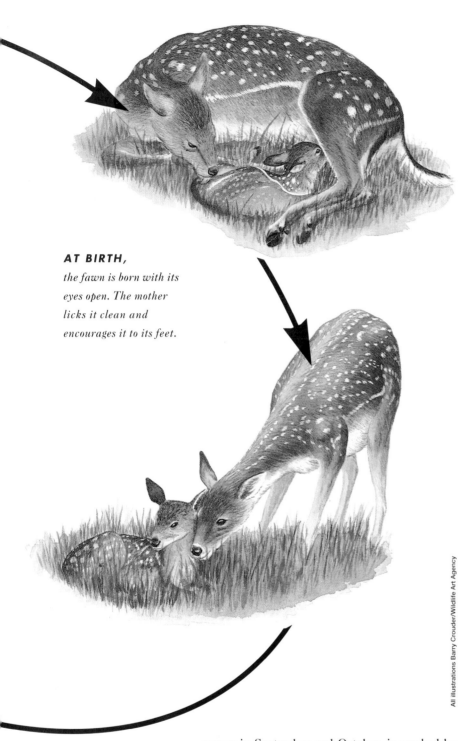

AT BIRTH,

the fawn is born with its eyes open. The mother licks it clean and encourages it to its feet.

THE FAWN

lies hidden in the undergrowth until it is able to run alongside its mother. She visits regularly to feed it.

All illustrations Barry Crouder/Wildlife Art Agency

small area that temporarily becomes his territory. He marks this by fraying tree trunks and marking them with scent from his facial glands, and scraping the ground with his antlers and urinating in the scrapes. He warns intruders to keep away by barking and prancing about on stiff legs. Fights occur only occasionally and are seldom serious, combat usually consisting of sparring with the antlers or boxing with the forelegs. Only if a senior buck is threatened by a close rival does a serious fight occur.

Normally, a younger buck signifies submission by giving a loud grunt and running away, and by the end of the rut an order of precedence will have

BOTH SEXES OF CARIBOU HAVE ANTLERS. THE LARGE BROW TINES ARE THOUGHT TO BE AN ADAPTATION TO PROTECT THE EYES FROM TWIGS AND STEMS OF BUSHES

been established. The younger bucks tend to have territories downwind or uphill of the older ones, who rush about trying to keep as many does as possible in their territories.

Red deer behave in a similar way. In October, the stags undergo a dramatic change of mood. They wallow in peaty bogs or muddy pools and roar or "bell" to each other and to the hinds. The hinds, which are sexually mature at three years old, are then rounded up into harems in areas about 100 ft (30 m) across, each dominated by a mature stag. The stags patrol their harems endlessly, roaring defiance at other stags and often engaging in fights. These fights are not merely sparring matches—foreheads clash and the antlers are used to inflict wounds. During a fight it is not uncommon for a

occurs in September and October, is marked by fighting between the bulls. They spar with their antlers, doing one another little or no damage, but the winners mate with more cows than the losers. Bulls bellow for the cows, and on hearing their answering calls, crash through the undergrowth to find them.

More territorial behavior is shown by fallow deer bucks. In October, each buck stakes out a

(in) SIGHT

RED ROAR

During the rut, red deer stags spend much of their time roaring at one another. A stag wishing to challenge another for possession of a harem approaches and begins to roar, and the incumbent stag roars back. Often the contest ends there or soon afterward, without a fight actually taking place. The

F. Millington/Planet Earth Pictures

reason for this can be seen in the cost of actually fighting. A mature stag fights about five times during the rut, and each time he does so, he risks considerable injury. In one study, it was found that 23 percent of stags were injured during the rut each year—up to 6 percent permanently. Thus any strategy that enables stags to establish dominance without fighting is an advantage. Stags appear to try to outdo their rivals in the frequency of their roars, and it has been shown that stags who can roar most often also tend to fare better in fights.

third stag to sneak swiftly into the harem and mate with one of the females, only to be chased off again as soon as the fight is over.

Gestation varies from about from 160 days in musk deer, 180 days in such species as muntjac, tufted deer, and white-tailed deer, to 280 or more days in roe deer and sambar. Roe deer take so long because implantation of the developing embyro is delayed until December in order that the young may be born the following May or June, when food is most plentiful.

Newly born deer are extremely vulnerable to predators and thus deer tend to be secretive about birth. A female roe deer produces her one or two (very occasionally three) fawns deep inside a thicket, and only brings them out after about a fortnight to rejoin the buck. The family group stays together at least until the end of the following winter, and male calves grow their first antlers, simple unbranched prongs, in February of their second year. Antlers increase in complexity until the fourth year, when they reach the full extent of their growth. In moose, the gestation period varies between 240 and 270 days and each cow normally produces two calves, except the first time, when she

produces only one. For the first three days the calves are unable to walk very much and the mother has to remain in close attendance. After about

CARIBOU CALVES, WHICH WEIGH ABOUT 9 LB (4 KG), CAN RUN AFTER HALF AN HOUR AND CAN OUTRUN A HUMAN AFTER FOUR HOURS

ten days the calves are able to run with their mother, and they remain together for two years.

Red deer produce their calves about 235 days after mating. Each hind chooses a secluded spot among the bracken and usually has a single calf. It can stand within a few minutes of being born and is able to run alongside its mother within a few hours. It is weaned after about nine months, but remains with the hind until the autumn of the following year. Young red deer become sexually mature between 15 and 28 months and may live for over 20 years. ■

All illustrations Robin Budden/Wildlife Art Agency

1. At the start of the contest, stags roar at each other for several minutes.

2. The two stags walk alongside each other until one turns to face the other.

3. The combatants lower their antlers, ready for combat.

4. The stags push strenuously, each trying to push the other rapidly backward.

AMAZING FACTS

William S. Paton/Planet Earth Pictures

● Mud wallowing is usually done to keep cool and/or to remove parasites.

● When danger threatens, fallow deer fawns freeze instinctively, making themselves almost invisible. Meanwhile the doe bolts in an attempt to draw a possible enemy away from her offspring.

SOCIAL STRUCTURE

Deer can be solitary or gregarious, depending on their circumstances. As in many mammal species, males tend to dominate and there is often, but by no means always, an established hierarchy among the males; and any males wishing to move up such a hierarchy must challenge others for their position.

The most gregarious deer are caribou and reindeer, which live in herds throughout the year. However, within these herds there is little evidence of any kind of hierarchy; there is no organization nor any established leader.

When necessary, a herd moves on as if by common agreement, and, if danger threatens, the members of the herd simply close up together. Axis deer also live in fairly large herds that consist of stags, hinds, and young of varying ages. Stags leave the herd only when they are about to shed their antlers.

Red deer, too, live in herds, but for most of the year stags live separately, either alone or in small

Mike Birkhead/Oxford Scientific Films

INSIGHT

In America, the Virginian, or white-tailed, deer live alone or in small family groups. In winter, food may be in short supply, and a party of up to 50 may gather in a "yard" to exploit a source of food. Snow is trampled and scraped away to expose the food underneath, and nearby trees may be severely damaged by browsing. When the food is exhausted, the group moves on.

The tail, which has the characteristic white underside, is raised when the animal flees, to signal impending danger.

groups, from the hinds. Communication between individuals is minimal, but a hind will sometimes bark or give a nasal bleat if alarmed. Even less frequently, a stag may produce a gruff bark. A distressed calf produces a high-pitched bleat. During the rut, on the other hand, a very definite social hierarchy exists among the stags; dominance is achieved only by the fittest, strongest stags with fully developed antlers.

Fallow deer occur most often today in parks, where small groups of does and groups of bucks can be seen at any time of year. In the wild, they are more solitary—for most of the time a doe lives

Muntjac are among the most solitary of deer. They rest in thickets during the day, coming out in the evening to feed. This muntjac is scent marking a tree.

Illustrations Wayne Ford/Wildlife Art Agency

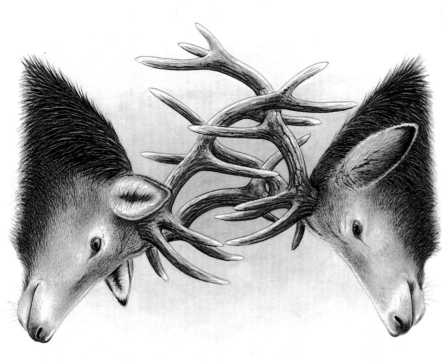

When two stags lock antlers, they risk more than just being pushed backward. When one tries to disengage, the other one is still pushing forward and, intentionally or not, may seriously injure the stag that is backing off. The tines on the antlers are sharp enough to penetrate skin if there is sufficient force behind them.

There is also another risk for both combatants. Occasionally, the antlers of two fighting stags become locked together, so that neither stag can disengage. When this happens, the inevitable result is that both stags starve to death.

The likelihood of the antlers themselves being damaged in a fight is very high. Antlers are shed and regrown every year—more or less leveling the playing field each new season.

PAMPAS DOES

Like many species of deer, the female pampas deer and their young live together.

with her fawn and the bucks live alone. In late autumn and early spring, however, groups of fallow deer come together in order to feed. Food is scarce during the winter, and if a good supply is found, all the nearby deer will take advantage of it. As with red deer, stags start to behave aggressively during the rut. By the end of the rut, successive confrontations will have established an order of precedence among the stags that by then is rarely challenged.

Roe deer never form herds. In winter they live in family groups of a buck, a doe, and her young. At the end of the winter, the young may be chased off, in time for the doe to produce her next young, but sometimes they remain in the group for several years. ∎

SCENT OF DEATH

HUNTED FOR FOOD, SPORT, OR, IN SOME CASES, FOR A SUBSTANCE ADDED TO PERFUME, THE WORLD DEER POPULATION NOW FACES AN EVEN GREATER PROBLEM THAN HUMANS—LOSS OF HABITAT

Deer have been hunted for their meat and hides since the Stone Age. Hunting continues today, and in parts of the United States deer are second only to the rabbit as the most hunted animal. As a result, the populations of some species have been diminished.

For many of the species that have survived, there is another problem. Deer, like all animal species, need the right type of habitat to survive. Most species prefer to live in forest or woodland—exactly the habitats that have been, and are being, cleared to make room for farmland. As a result, a number of species are under threat because their habitat is disappearing, and several subspecies are almost certainly now extinct.

In this, of course, deer are not alone; habitat destruction is now the greatest single threat to wildlife species throughout the world. Of all living species of deer, 29 subspecies are listed by the IUCN as being endangered or vulnerable, and the

Discarded fishing lines can be a very real danger to deer grazing near lakes and rivers.

Toward autumn, food starts getting scarce, and many of the young may die in winter.

Nick Garbutt/Planet Earth Pictures

MEASURES HAVE BEEN TAKEN TO PROTECT SUCH DEER AS THE COLUMBIAN WHITE-TAILED DEER AND THE CEDROS ISLAND MULE DEER

---

list includes 12 full species. Curiously, only one species, *Cervus schombergki*, which was last recorded in Thailand in 1932, has become extinct during the last 100 years; but there is no reason for complacency, since it would seem that a number of others could become extinct in the very near future.

The effect of overhunting, or overexploitation as it is often called, can be illustrated by what happened to wapiti, or elk, populations in the Yellowstone area of Wyoming. Intense hunting during the 19th century reduced numbers to a dangerously low level

by the mid-1880s, and although hunting in Yellowstone Park was prohibited in 1883, the population was so low that the process of recovery was slow. By 1930, however, the number of wapiti had risen again, to between 12,000 and 16,000, and the park authorities once again began to issue hunting permits to shoot them. The result was perhaps inevitable; for one reason or another, controls were not enforced and wapiti were again overhunted, and by 1968 the population had once again fallen, to around 4,000. A moratorium on all hunting in the park was imposed in 1969, and since then the numbers have risen satisfactorily.

Deer are hunted in most parts of the world, but they are not necessarily hunted just for their meat and hides. Antlers are popular as trophies, and in parts of eastern Asia deer are hunted because their

Stan Osolinski/Oxford Scientific Films

antlers are used in the medicine trade. McNeill's deer of Chinese Turkistan and Thorolds deer of eastern Tibet and China are both of unknown status at present; McNeill's deer may well be extinct. The population of the Himalayan musk deer has been greatly depleted primarily because of hunting; the animal is prized for the musk that the male produces in pouches on its belly. The musk deer is not as yet endangered, since it is estimated that there is still a viable population of between 25,000 and

---

A PROFITABLE INDUSTRY MIGHT BE STARTED BY FARMING MUSK DEER, SINCE IT IS NOT NECESSARY TO KILL THE DEER IN ORDER TO EXTRACT ITS MUSK

30,000 individuals. However, if hunting pressure continues, the situation may well deteriorate.

The wapiti, or elk, story is, perhaps, a little unusual, as it is rare for hunting alone to affect the population of a deer species so dramatically. In such cases it is probably the restricted nature of suitable habitat, combined with extremely high hunting pressure, that causes numbers to decline. In contrast, where deer

DEER IN DANGER

THE CHART BELOW SHOWS HOW THE INTERNATIONAL UNION FOR THE CONSERVATION OF NATURE (IUCN), OR WORLD CONSERVATION UNION, LISTS THE FOLLOWING SPECIES AS HAVING CONSERVATION CONCERN:

THESE SPECIES ARE LISTED AS ENDANGERED:

FEA'S MUNTJAC
SWAMP DEER
MULE DEER
WHITE-TAILED DEER
PAMPAS DEER

THESE SPECIES ARE LISTED AS VULNERABLE:

CALAMIAN DEER
MARSH DEER
PERUVIAN HUEMUL

ENDANGERED MEANS THAT THE ANIMAL'S SURVIVAL IS UNLIKELY UNLESS STEPS ARE TAKEN TO SAVE IT. VULNERABLE INDICATES THAT THE ANIMAL IS LIKELY TO MOVE INTO THE ENDANGERED CATEGORY FOR SPECIES CONTAINING SUBSPECIES IN DIFFERENT CATEGORIES.

ALONGSIDE MAN

DEER AS PESTS

Any species present in such large numbers that it causes damage to crops or the environment is regarded as a pest, and some deer come into this category. Red deer were introduced to New Zealand and rapidly increased to such numbers that government control programs were introduced. In Europe during the winter and early spring, roe deer feed on crops when there is little for them to eat in the woods. One way of reducing this is to plant and maintain grassy feeding areas within the woods, and supply the deer with mineral and sugar licks.

R. Sorenson and J. Olsen/NHPA

become so numerous that they are regarded as a pest species, it has proved somewhat difficult to reduce their population satisfactorily. In fact, culling deer extensively can exacerbate the problem by causing the remaining deer to spread into new areas where they feel safer, and even changing their behavior so that they become more difficult to find.

In most cases overhunting is only one of the factors that have contributed to the decline of deer species. In its native habitat, the mountainous evergreen forests of Burma and Thailand, Fea's muntjac has declined due to habitat destruction exacerbated by hunting. Its current status is not known. Numbers of the Yarkand deer—a subspecies of red deer native to Xinjiang district of Chinese Turkistan—have been reduced not only by heavy hunting but also by large areas of its native riverine forest having been lost to agriculture. Its status, too, is currently unknown, and it may well be extinct. It is estimated that the number of Argentinian pampas deer has been reduced to a mere 200 individuals, again due to a combination of overhunting and loss of habitat to agriculture. This species is further

In some areas moose are regarded as pests and are shot by farmers trying to protect their crops.

This European moose has found sanctuary from farmers in a wildlife park.

Terry Mayes/Planet Earth Pictures

Lon. E. Lauber/Oxford Scientific Films

Deer need to rub their antlers on trees in order to shed skin. However, this practice can adversely affect shrunken habitats by causing widespread damage to trees.

AMAZING FACTS

MUSK FOR PERFUME

Male musk deer have pouches on their bellies in which they produce an exudate known as musk, a highly prized substance that is used as a fixative for perfume. Musk is a valuable commodity and hence musk deer have been hunted for many years. During the 1930s, between 10,000 and 15,000 musk deer were killed each year, with the inevitable result that numbers were greatly reduced. Today, the harvesting of musk for commercial purposes is prohibited in China, unless special permission is obtained. However, poaching continues, and the population of alpine musk deer is known to be decreasing.

threatened by competition with domestic livestock that are grazed on its native range. It also suffers from the same diseases carried by domestic animals.

Other deer endangered through a combination of overhunting and habitat removal include the Thailand brow-antlered deer, the Formosan sika, the Corsican red deer, and the Kasmir deer, or hangul. The Calamian deer of the Philippines is classed as vulnerable, but may soon be endangered as numbers are estimated at 900 and declining. The Peruvian huemels and the marsh deer are both protected to some extent but are still declining due to poaching as well as loss of habitat. ∎

INTO THE FUTURE

Assuming that no major disaster befalls the world, there will always be deer; as we have seen, some species are remarkably good survivors. However, it does seem likely that, if present trends continue, the number of species of deer will be somewhat reduced.

Conservation measures are easy enough to enact, if governments are willing, but are not necessarily

PREDICTION

DOOMED TO EXTINCTION

If it still exists, the Manipur brow-antlered deer, or sangai, the world's most endangered deer, is probably doomed to extinction. Only a few individuals remain in a national park in Manipur, India.

so easy to enforce. For example, the South Andean huemul is protected by law in Chile, but in practice it is difficult to prevent hunters from carrying on their trade. The marsh deer is also protected throughout its range, but enforcement is lacking in all of the countries in which it is found.

Similar situations exist in many Asian countries, where local peoples may simply ignore bans on hunting, either because it is part of a tradition or, more often, because the possibility of financial gain outweighs the possible penalties. And, of course, as human populations increase and people's expectations of their standard of living grow ever higher, the process of economic development often supersedes environmental considerations. Vital habitats are often destroyed, for example, to make room for roads, dams, and housing, thus threatening not only deer but a whole range of species. ■

PREDICTION

GOING HOME

In 1986 a group of Père David's deer, which are extinct in the wild, were brought back to their native region—the swampy plains of northern China. It is hoped that the species will be reintroduced into the wild.

DEER FARMING

Hans Reinhard/Bruce Coleman Ltd.

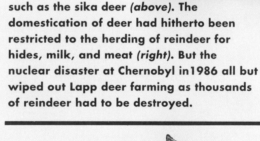

Anup Char/Planet Earth Pictures

The last thirty years have seen an increase in deer farming in Britain, Australia, and New Zealand, both as a means of food production and for the conservation of endangered species, such as the sika deer *(above)*. The domestication of deer had hitherto been restricted to the herding of reindeer for hides, milk, and meat *(right)*. But the nuclear disaster at Chernobyl in 1986 all but wiped out Lapp deer farming as thousands of reindeer had to be destroyed.

Illustration Kim Thompson

DHOLES

David Curl/Oxford Scientific Films

The dhole, dingo, and raccoon dog are distantly related members of the dog family, Canidae, which includes all the dogs, wolves, jackals, and foxes. The family Canidae is one of seven in the order Carnivora, a group of mainly predatory mammals distinguished by their meat-slicing carnassial teeth.

ORDER

Carnivora
(carnivores)

FAMILY

Canidae
(dogs)

GENUS & SPECIES

Cuon alpinus
(dhole)

Canis familiaris dingo
(dingo)

Nyctereutes procyonoides
(raccoon dog)

CANIDS WITH CUNNING

HAILING FROM DIFFERENT REGIONS, AND WITH LITTLE IN COMMON AS TO THEIR APPEARANCE, THE DHOLE, DINGO (*ABOVE*), AND RACCOON DOG NEVERTHELESS ALL EXHIBIT TYPICALLY CANINE GUILE AND VERSATILITY

S oon after dawn, deep within the tiger forests of the Ranthambhore National Park in Rajasthan, northern India, a group of wild dogs gathers in the long, lush grass of a clearing. Trotting easily on long, slender legs, their coats glowing red in the morning sun, they look like big, playful foxes as they nuzzle and greet each other. They have the same lithe, lightweight look as foxes; the same pricked-up ears lined with white fur; the same dark bushy tails.

Yet they are not foxes. Their faces have shorter, much broader jaws. They are the jaws of extremely efficient carnivores. These graceful wild dogs are dholes: possibly the most murderously efficient killers to be found throughout the whole of Asia.

A dhole on its own poses little threat. Its teeth may be more forbidding than those of most wild dogs, but they cannot compare with the daggerlike canines of a tiger or leopard. It also lacks the sheer muscle of the big cats—muscle that enables a lone

575

tiger to ambush and strangle the life from an ox. Like most canids, the dhole is built for running, with long legs; small, well-padded feet with blunt, fixed claws for traction; and a deep chest to provide the lung capacity and stamina for a sustained, fast chase.

PACK HUNTERS

Lupine (wolflike) canids developed these traits in response to climatic changes that began some five to six million years ago—changes that favored the development of grasslands and the fleet-footed antelope, deer, and other hoofed animals that grazed them. But by specializing in pursuit, rather than ambush, the lupines sacrificed the brawn that might enable them to subdue big animals single-handed, and any wild dogs that prefer to hunt big game have had to learn to pool their resources and share the spoils. The dhole is just such a cooperative killer, so while a solitary individual may be barely more formidable than the fox it resembles, it is a very different proposition when it is hunting with the pack.

Of the thirty-five species in the dog family Canidae, only three are dedicated pack-hunting predators of large animals: the African hunting dog, the little-known bush dog of Amazonia, and, of course, the dhole of Asia. They also have similarities in their teeth. In most dogs the carnassial (shearing) teeth have blades at the front and grinding surfaces at the back, but in the dhole, hunting dog, and bush dog the carnassials have slicing blades front and rear, like those of a cat. Meat is easily digested, so it can be swallowed in chunks; since a dhole eats very little else, it has little reason to chew its food, and therefore little need for chewing teeth.

Terry Whittaker/Frank Lane Picture Agency

R. Bender/Frank Lane Picture Agency

The raccoon dog is about the size of its namesake, and has the facial markings to match (above).

A TOOTHY DEBATE

Teeth are often all that is left of prehistoric animals whose bones have long since crumbled to dust. For this reason they are extremely useful to scientists, and many extinct species have been described on the basis of their teeth alone.

Until recently the dhole, African wild dog, and bush dog were classified in a subfamily of their own because their carnassial teeth are similar: a bladelike cusp at the back instead of a flat surface. This classification may be perfectly valid, but it is also possible that the three species evolved the feature independently. Similar examples of "parallel evolution" are accepted as common in nature, but the idea that the principle can be extended to teeth has loosened a few deep-rooted assumptions.

The dhole's distant ancestors were more adaptable, for their teeth could process a wide range of foods. Many modern canids, such as the foxes, have inherited this flexibility, but few are more omnivorous than the dhole's curious canine neighbor in Asia, the raccoon dog. A more startling contrast with the dhole could hardly be imagined, for while the dhole is an elegant, leggy athlete, the raccoon dog is a portly, heavily furred creature with short legs and a narrow muzzle. As its name suggests, it looks more like a raccoon than a dog—chiefly because of the raccoonlike bandit mask across its eyes—and it also behaves more like a raccoon than a dog, devouring seeds, fruits, insects, birds, and small mammals with equal relish.

The origins of the raccoon dog are obscure. It has no close living relatives, and it probably evolved from an offshoot of the Canidae that diverged from the mainstream some six million years ago, before the canid line split into the lupine dogs and the vulpine foxes. It certainly has few obvious affinities with either the lean, rangy dogs or the delicate, almost catlike foxes. Yet despite being something of an evolutionary sideline, it has flourished in the Asian forests, as well as throughout much of eastern Europe following its artificial introduction as a fur-bearer in 1928. The legacy of its primitive ancestry has probably served it well, since its very lack of specialized features has enabled it to adapt to a wide variety of foods and habitats.

The dhole is a curious blend of fox and wolf: It has the looks of the former and the habits of the latter.

By contrast, the Australian dingo almost certainly has its origins in the most recent canid offshoot—the domestic dog. It was probably introduced from New Guinea by humans some 4,000–8,000 years ago, possibly as a pet or working dog of some kind, and has since gone native. Dingolike dogs are still to be found in New Guinea and nearby islands, where they are semidomesticated. The New Guinea singing dog—named for its curiously musical vocalizations—looks like a smaller version of the dingo and may be descended from a common ancestor, but there is no hard evidence for this, since the earliest fossil remains of the singing dog are only 1,500 years old. The origins of the ancestral domestic dog itself are even less clear, but they are probably to be found in the small Indian race of the gray wolf.

Whatever its ancestry, the dingo has prospered in its adopted land, growing larger than its New Guinea cousins on the rich variety of prey and colonizing

THE CANIDS' FAMILY TREE

Although dogs are universally familiar, the relationships between the various species are still uncertain. However, the often-conflicting evidence inferred from their anatomy and behavior is now being clarified by genetic studies, and ultimately this may clear up any remaining doubts about their ancestry.

JACKALS

COYOTE

Color illustrations Barry Croucher/Wildlife Art Agency

DHOLE
Cuon alpinus
(KEW-on al-PINE-us)

The dhole is a long-legged hunting dog that has specialized in bringing down large prey using pack tactics, and has unusually powerful jaws and teeth. It hunts through forest and thick scrub, maintaining contact with whistling calls that have earned it the name "whistling hunter." Elusive and mysterious, it is now rare in many areas as a result of the destruction of its forest habitat.

almost every habitat, from the deserts of the interior to the subtropical forests of northern Queensland. Like the dhole it is built for running and has a reputation as a pack hunter, but typically it forages alone for small and medium-sized prey. The introduction of sheep to the Australian grasslands in the late 18th century provided rich pickings for a while, but the resulting persecution has driven it into the outback. Its subsequent elusiveness and dubious origins have discouraged scientific interest in its habits, and so, paradoxically, the once-domestic dingo remains one of the most mysterious of all wild dogs. ∎

VULPINES (FOXLIKE)

VULPINE FOXES

ALL DOGS (CANIDAE)

WOLF

DINGO

Canis familiaris dingo
(CAN-is fam-ill-ee-AH-riss
DIN-go)

Introduced to Australia by humans at least 4,000 years ago, the dingo is an early form of domestic dog that has returned to the wild. A descendant of the gray wolf, it has inherited the wolf's adaptability and opportunist habits—a legacy that enabled it to spread throughout the varied habitats of Australia until persecution by humans drove it into the remotest regions of the continent.

AFRICAN
WILD DOG

MANED WOLF AND
SOUTH AMERICAN FOXES

B/W illustrations Ruth Grewcock; Coyote Kim Thompson

LUPINES
(WOLFLIKE)

RACCOON DOG

Nyctereutes
procyonoides
(nick-ter-ROYT-eez
pro-sy-on-OY-deez)

This unusual dog has ancient origins and probably lives in much the same way as the earliest canids, foraging through the forest for small animals, insects, and fruit. It lives among dense undergrowth and is unique among canids because it passes the winter in a form of hibernation in the northern parts of its range.

ANATOMY:
THE DHOLE

THE EARS

are large and sensitive, enabling the dhole to detect hidden prey and also keep track of its companions in dense undergrowth with its soft whistling calls.

THE EYES

have a wide field of view, which is essential for a hunter, but their frontal position also provides the binocular vision that enables distances to be judged accurately for the final strike. A reflective membrane behind the retina of each eye increases its sensitivity in low light.

Largest of the three, the dingo (above left) is slightly smaller than a typical gray wolf. The dhole (above center) stands almost as tall as the dingo, but is more compact in form. The raccoon dog (above right) is about the size and weight of a common raccoon.

THE MUZZLE

is shorter and broader than that of most dogs, but is still long enough to contain keen sensory apparatus. The damp, leathery surface moistens the inhaled air and increases the nose's scent-carrying capacity.

FOREFOOT

The dhole's feet are small and compact, with well-cushioned pads that act as shock absorbers when the animal is running fast on hard surfaces, and sturdy, blunt, nonretractable claws for improved traction. Dewclaws on the forelimbs stay sharp because they are not in contact with the ground, and may help the dhole subdue small prey. Only domestic dogs—and dingoes—have dewclaws on the hind limbs.

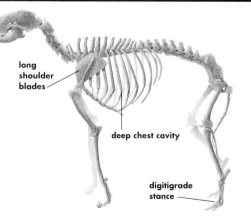

X-RAY

DHOLE SKELETON
Like most dogs, the dhole has a strong but relatively inflexible spine and a deep chest cavity to contain capacious lungs for stamina. Its limbs are extended for speed by elongated shoulder blades and a digitigrade stance (it runs on its toes). The bones of the lower limbs are fused together for strength.

long shoulder blades

deep chest cavity

digitigrade stance

CARNASSIAL TEETH
The lower carnassials of the dhole have two sharp cusps in line. These act against the upper carnassials like scissor blades to shear through tough hide, sinew, and flesh. In most other dogs, such as the dingo, each lower carnassial has two rear cusps that form a grinding surface, suiting a broader diet.

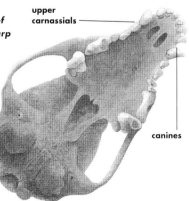

upper carnassials

canines

X-ray illustrations Elisabeth Smith

DHOLE

The dhole has a short, broad muzzle, and its ears have rounded tips.

DINGO

The dingo has the clean, elegant facial features characteristic of the lupine canids.

RACCOON DOG

The raccoon dog has a full, bushy coat, small, rounded ears, and a face mask—just like that of a real raccoon.

FACT FILE:

DHOLE

CLASSIFICATION

GENUS: *CUON*

SPECIES: *ALPINUS*

SIZE

HEAD–BODY LENGTH: 35 IN (90 CM)

TAIL LENGTH: 16–18 IN (40–45 CM)

AVERAGE WEIGHT: 37 LB (17 KG)

NORTHERN ANIMALS ARE SOME 20 PERCENT LARGER THAN OTHERS

COLORATION

VARIES FROM BROWN GRAY TO MAHOGANY RED, OFTEN WITH BLACK-TIPPED FUR ON THE BACK. TAIL IS BLACK AND BUSHY, ALTHOUGH OCCASIONALLY THE TAIL HAS WHITE FUR. MANY INDIVIDUALS HAVE A WHITE THROAT PATCH THAT MAY EXTEND DOWN THE CHEST

FEATURES

LITHE, SLENDER BUILD

LONG, SLIM LEGS

DARK BUSHY TAIL

BROAD MUZZLE

ERECT, ROUNDED EARS

THE BUSHY TAIL

with its black-tipped fur is used like a semaphore flag to signal states of arousal and social submission. It also helps the dhole keep its balance when running fast.

THE THICK PELT

has a woolly undercoat to protect the dhole against the winter cold in the north of its range. The coat is less dense farther south, but often a deeper red: In India the dhole is sometimes known as the red dog.

THE SLENDER LEGS

are well muscled throughout their length to provide the strength for subduing prey as well as running.

SKULL

The dhole has a shorter, broader jaw than a wolf, so the canine teeth are nearer to the jaw hinge: This increases their biting power. The shortened jawline means that the dhole has lost one molar tooth on each side of the lower jaw, but since it rarely needs to chew its food into smaller, more manageable morsels, this is a small sacrifice.

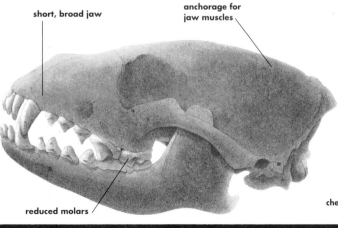

short, broad jaw

anchorage for jaw muscles

reduced molars

JAW MUSCLES

One set of jaw muscles attaches to the large crest at the back of the skull, while the other set lies beneath the cheekbone.

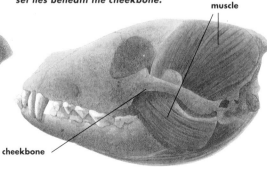

muscle

cheekbone

PACK HUNTERS

THE PACK-HUNTING DHOLES OF THE EASTERN FORESTS CAN SUBDUE POWERFUL PREY THAT WOULD DAUNT A TIGER, BUT OTHER DOGS, LIKE THE DINGO AND THE RACCOON DOG, PREFER A QUIETER LIFE

Bushy tails raised high in anticipation, ears pricked forward to catch the slightest rustle in the dense forest undergrowth, five red-coated dholes methodically pick their way toward a clearing in search of prey. They are on the alert, but they are not taking care to conceal themselves. The odd snapping twig or even a whiff of wild dog carried into the scrub ahead of them will do no harm at all, for their object is not to catch the prey but to scare it. Like beaters flushing pheasants for the guns, they hope to spook their victims into a headlong rush in the opposite direction, into the clearing and into the jaws of the rest of the hunting group, lurking in ambush in the long grass. It is a simple maneuver, but it depends on effective coordination between the hunters—coordination that is possible only between highly social animals that have refined the art of running with the pack.

WORKING TOGETHER

As a specialist at hunting big, powerful animals that it would not risk tackling alone, the dhole relies on strength of numbers. Yet while the actual kill may be simply a matter of maximizing the number of active teeth to ensure a quick, efficient job, the lead-up to the kill often requires each animal to play a specific role, secure in the knowledge that it will get its share of the spoils. This involves the kind of mutual trust and communication that can only develop between animals that live together in the tight bond of an extended family—a way of life that naturally influences every element of the dhole's behavior. Its territoriality, body language, food preferences, breeding strategy, and ultimately its ability to thrive in humankind's world are all determined by its compulsively social nature. The dhole has become a specialist at group living, and in the process it has developed into a pack predator.

Most other canids have retained a more adaptable approach, and although this may limit their ability to carry out subtle group-hunting tactics, it has the advantage of flexibility. The dingo is a prime example of this. Australian folklore depicts it as a pack hunter with all the cunning and ferocity of the dhole, but in reality it is an opportunist that tailors its behavior to suit its situation. This may involve forming packs in some areas, with all the social and predatory consequences, but at the other extreme it may lead to the low-profile lifestyle of a solitary forager for small game and scraps, more reminiscent of a fox or a coyote. Such a way of life is particularly appropriate for an animal that suffers relentless persecution, since it often enables it to live virtually unnoticed by its human neighbors. The red fox, for example, has managed to extend its range into city centers by adopting this way of life. The dingo is elusive to the point of invisibility—something that would not be the case if it typically hunted over the

Dingoes are adaptable enough to use pack tactics when an opportunity presents itself (above).

W. Weisser/Ardea

Jean Paul Ferrero/Ardea

 **SIGHT**

WINTER RETREAT

The raccoon dog is the only member of the dog family that hibernates in winter. Hibernation is not simply an extended snooze: It involves a slowing down of the animal's metabolic rate, which reduces body temperature and therefore energy consumption. The animal sinks into a state of torpor while its life support systems function on standby, and if it needs to move, it may use a lot of energy simply warming itself up to get its body functioning.

The object of hibernation is not to avoid the winter weather but to survive a food shortage by cutting energy consumption. Insect-eating animals that have their food supply wiped out by low temperatures tend to stay in a state of deep torpor throughout the winter, but as an omnivore the raccoon dog does not have to take such extreme measures. Its hibernation is relatively shallow, its metabolism moves along at a good pace, and it may wake up to feed quite frequently. In the south of its range it may not hibernate at all, but keep active throughout the year.

open grasslands in big packs—and this is one of the main reasons why it remains relatively common.

The social adaptability of the dingo does not seem to be shared by the raccoon dog. As a small omnivore it has nothing to gain from associating in hunting groups, and no reason to range over a large group territory. It can find all it needs within a relatively small area, feeding either alone or in pairs, and it tends to keep to thick vegetation where it can forage unseen, at night. Raccoon dogs have plenty of enemies, including eagles, owls, lynxes, and other wild dogs such as wolves and even dholes, so its behavior is strongly influenced by the need to stay out of trouble.

By contrast, the dhole has no natural enemies and normally hunts by day, when it can take advantage of its keen eyesight. The dingo may also be active by day, depending on the habits of its prey, but like many wild animals it has learned to lie low during the daylight hours, particularly if there are people around. The dingo's ancestors may have enjoyed the privileges of being humankind's best friend, but that day has long gone. ■

Like all canids, the dhole has superb senses, and is alert to the slightest sounds of prey or enemies.

HABITATS

The lupine dogs evolved to exploit the hoofed grazing animals of the grassy plains, but as pack hunters they have always been most effective in scrub country, where the concealing vegetation allows them to get close to their quarry and outmaneuver it without wasting energy in a long chase. Wolves frequently hunt in open forests, and the dhole has become a specialist at flushing prey from cover, cutting off its retreat, and closing for the kill before it can make a break for open country. This has enabled it to flourish throughout the forests of southern and eastern Asia as well as the open plains—indeed, it is usually considered a forest animal, and the largest surviving dhole populations occur in the forested wildlife reserves of north India.

FOREST SURVIVOR

"Surviving" is the critical word, for at one time the dhole had a far wider range than it has today. Fossil dhole remains have been found in Europe, indicating that it once roamed throughout much of the Eurasian landmass. Even now it is one of the most widely distributed canids in Asia, for, although many populations have been reduced to threadbare remnants by persecution, it is to be found from the

Dingoes greet each other affectionately in the dry, dusty Australian interior.

cold northern conifer forests to the steamy tropical jungles of Sumatra and Java.

Like its relative the gray wolf, the dhole has a broad temperature tolerance, and is particularly well equipped to survive cold conditions. This enables it to thrive both in the Siberian forests, which regularly experience arctic levels of frost, and on the Himalayas and the Tibetan plateau. Dholes living in such areas have much longer, thicker winter coats than their more-pampered counterparts in the southern lowlands, and are some 20 percent larger. Bigger animals have a greater mass in proportion to their skin area, which reduces the rate at which they lose heat; accordingly, many species display an increase in size in cold climates. Arctic wolves, for example, are on average twice the weight of Arabian wolves. The size range of the dhole is not so extreme, but neither is its habitat range.

In Thailand the dhole survives best in mountain forests rising more than 9,840 ft (3,000 m) above sea level, but in India it flourishes in river valleys in protected areas. The only habitat it seems to avoid is desert, and for this reason it is absent from large tracts of central Asia including much of Mongolia and northern China. Its disappearance from eastern China, however, has more to do with the destruction of wild habitats by the vast human population than any climatic constraint.

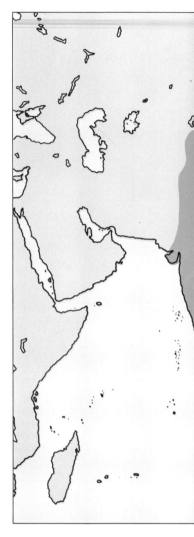

Martin Harry/NHPA

in SIGHT

OUT OF TASMANIA

The arrival of the dingo in Australia spelled trouble for the native wildlife—not only prey like wallabies and bandicoots but also the native marsupial predators. The most spectacular of these was the Tasmanian wolf, a large, doglike creature whose fossils have been found throughout mainland Australia. The Tasmanian wolf appears to have retreated as the dingo advanced, and by the time Europeans arrived in Australia, it had disappeared completely from the mainland, but was still thriving on the dingo-free island refuge of Tasmania.

Tasmania is still dingo-free, but, sadly for the Tasmanian wolf, it attracted sheep farmers in the early 19th century. The Tasmanian wolf was ruthlessly persecuted as a suspected sheep killer, and by the late 1930s had apparently been wiped out altogether.

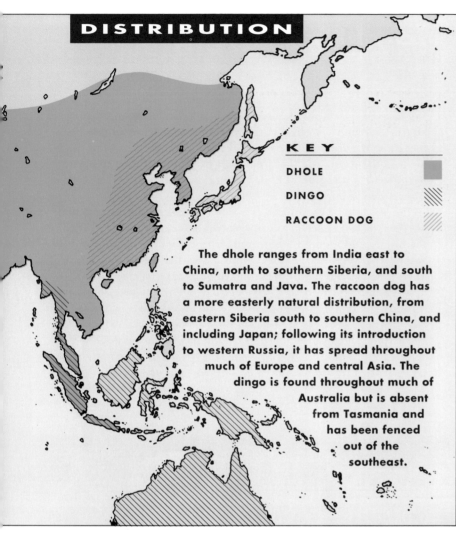

DISTRIBUTION

KEY

DHOLE

DINGO

RACCOON DOG

The dhole ranges from India east to China, north to southern Siberia, and south to Sumatra and Java. The raccoon dog has a more easterly natural distribution, from eastern Siberia south to southern China, and including Japan; following its introduction to western Russia, it has spread throughout much of Europe and central Asia. The dingo is found throughout much of Australia but is absent from Tasmania and has been fenced out of the southeast.

The same environmental degradation affects the raccoon dog, which was originally found in woodlands and forests from southeastern Siberia and Manchuria to northern Vietnam, as well as on the main islands of Japan. But as a small, secretive animal prepared to take a wide range of foods, it needs less space than the dhole and attracts less adverse attention, so it has remained widespread except in the most heavily developed areas. In its natural environment it generally keeps to heavily wooded regions with dense undergrowth—preferably ferns—often close to lakes and streams, but its foxlike opportunism has enabled it to exploit a variety of unlikely habitats. Raccoon dogs frequently gather to scavenge from village garbage dumps, and on the coast they pick their way along the beach searching for stranded fish and other morsels among the rotting debris cast up on the shoreline.

RUSSIAN RACCOON DOG RELEASE

The adaptability of the raccoon dog has enabled it to expand its range far beyond its original distribution in eastern Asia. Between 1928 and 1957 some 9,000 raccoon dogs were released into the wild in various parts of western Russia in the hope of creating flourishing populations of valuable fur-bearing animals. In this respect the project was a failure, since, for some unknown reason, its fur did not grow as long as in the east, but the raccoon dog took to its new

A pair of dholes test the air for signs of prey in the clearing of an Indian forest.

Anup Shah/Planet Earth Pictures

environment with great enthusiasm and spread through European Russia, much of Scandinavia, and central Europe. It now occurs throughout Germany and has crossed the border into France. By 1984 it was estimated that the raccoon dog had spread over an area of 540,000 sq mi (1,400,000 sq km) since its introduction to the West in 1928.

NO-GO FOR DINGOES

The dingo achieved similar success in Australia, but so long ago that there is no record of its rate of spread. At the time of the European colonization, it was found throughout the continent—on the plains, among mountain ranges, and in the extensive eucalypt woodlands and northern rain forests, where it fed on a variety of prey ranging from insects to kangaroos. Inevitably, fears of dingo attacks on sheep led to its persecution and expulsion from the richer grazing lands, a process that culminated in the erection of the astonishing "dog fence" which, with a length of 3,488 mi (5,614 km), is two-and-a-half times as long as the Great Wall of China. Cutting off the whole of New South Wales, Victoria, and about half the state of South Australia, the fence has not proved inviolate; however, it helps to keep the dingo and its only enemy apart, and possibly benefits the dog by reducing the need for lethal control.

Meanwhile the eviction of the dingo from the southeast was in some way balanced by the introduction of the European rabbit, which multiplied to plague numbers within a few years of its Australian debut in 1859. Despite the onslaught of the disease myxomatosis in the 1950s, the rabbit is still a pest in Australia, and it provides the dingo with an endless supply of food, even in the interior. Today both rabbit and dingo flourish in the scorched outback of their adopted land, forming their own "ecosystem" in one of the most remote wildernesses on earth. ■

FOCUS ON

USSURILAND

The luxuriant pelt of the raccoon dog is known to some furriers as "Ussuri raccoon" in reference to the animal's stronghold in the forests of Ussuriland in eastern Siberia. Lying between the Amur River in the north and the great port of Vladivostok in the south, Ussuriland is a region of high mountains, broad plains, and dense forests bordering the Sea of Japan.

The wildlife of Ussuriland is a rich mixture of subtropical and northern forest species, exemplified by spectacular predators like the highly endangered Siberian tiger and Amur leopard—both of southern origin—and the brown bear and the wolverine, which have invaded the region from the taiga forests of the north.

The region also has a sparse population of dholes, who hunt through the mixed forests for wild boar, wild goats, red deer, and the rare sika deer, as well as smaller residents such as Manchurian hares and Siberian chipmunks. Raccoon dogs are relatively common in the river valleys, where they forage for fruit on the forest floor and hunt small game such as rodents, lizards, and frogs, gorging themselves in autumn to accumulate enough stored energy to see them through their long winter sleep.

Darek Karp/NHPA

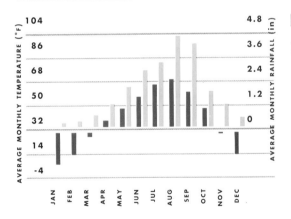

TEMPERATURE AND RAINFALL

■ TEMPERATURE
▪ RAINFALL

Ussuriland is gripped by a bitter subzero Siberian climate during winter. In these dry, cold conditions, rainfall is minimal. Summer brings a warm, moist respite, owing to the prevailing winds that blow in from the Pacific.

NEIGHBORS

At the end of the last Ice Age, the Ussuriland region was invaded by animals from steppe, forest, tropical, mountain, and Siberian regions, giving rise to the rich range of fauna found there today.

ASIAN BLACK BEAR

This small bear is a shy inhabitant of forest and brush regions. It feeds on nuts, fruit, and insects.

TIGER SNAKE

The tiger snake is an amphibious predator that includes fire-bellied toads in its broad diet.

THE FAR EAST

Ussuriland lies in the far east of Russia. It borders on China to the south and west, while to the east lies the Sea of Japan. Sakhalin, which lies close off the northeast coast, is part of the "ring of fire"—a chain of volcanic islands that includes Japan.

USSURILAND

MERGANSER

The red-breasted merganser is widespread across Europe and Asia, from Britain to Japan.

ALTAI WEASEL

Also known as the yellow-throated marten, this mustelid is a fierce and adept little predator.

FIRE-BELLIED TOAD

The bright markings of the eastern fire-bellied toad warn would-be predators of its toxic secretions.

GIANT SILK MOTH

The silk itself is spun in one long fiber by the larva to form the cocoon in which it undergoes metamorphosis.

FISHING OWL

Blakiston's fishing owl is highly skilled at scooping fish from surface waters with its talons.

HUNTING

Padding softly across the desert in the noon sun, a dingo pauses to sniff at a rabbit hole. It listens intently, then passes on to the next hole, and the next. This time it stops dead and stays stock-still for a minute or two, before pouncing upon the hole in a flurry of dust. After a squeal and a snap it emerges triumphant, a rabbit hanging limp in its jaws.

The introduction of the rabbit to Australia in the mid-19th century was a godsend to the dingo. After several millennia spent chasing increasingly scarce marsupial prey, it was presented with a furry feast: an exploding population of fast food. Yet the rabbit was no easy meal. Genetically programmed to bolt for cover at the slightest alarm, it presented quite a challenge to the dingo's hunting skills. As a born opportunist, however, the dingo swiftly found ways of dealing with it. When rabbits are feeding actively in the cool of the early morning or evening, a dingo may stalk them, creeping silently through long grass or scrub until it is close enough to strike. More

> DINGOES ACTIVELY PATROL RABBIT WARRENS, IN THE HOPE OF CATCHING AN INEXPERIENCED YOUNGSTER IN THE OPEN

commonly it relies on sheer speed, hurling itself at a feeding group and snatching any animal briefly disoriented by the panic.

Canids are typically versatile when it comes to hunting; dingoes will take almost any prey, from grasshoppers to gray kangaroos, although they feed mainly on medium-sized mammals such as rabbits and wallabies. In Asia the raccoon dog concentrates on smaller prey such as rodents, frogs, and lizards, and can even deal with toxic toads by smothering the acrid secretions of their skin glands with quantities of saliva. It also eats a lot of fruit, particularly in the period before winter; rangy raccoon dogs cannot hibernate for fear of starving before spring, and are forced to keep active throughout the winter months.

COOPERATIVE KILLING

Dingoes in quest of kangaroos and other big game may form packs, but the real expert at this type of high-risk hunting is the dhole. The risks are high because a powerful animal such as a chital stag, or axis deer, or a gray kangaroo can disembowel a dog with a single well-aimed kick; on the other hand, the rewards of a successful kill are considerable, with food in plenty for the whole hunting pack and any hungry pups that may be waiting hopefully at the den.

(in) SIGHT

PIRACY!

Dingoes regularly scavenge the kills of wedge-tailed eagles, crunching through the skin and bones discarded by the birds. They keep an eye on hunting eagles, and given the chance, a dingo may well steal an eagle's kill before it has finished with it.

In India dholes may pirate the kills of leopards and tigers, and if they get the chance, the leopards and tigers will return the compliment. But dholes are tough customers, quite capable of killing a tiger that tries to make off with their meal.

Illustrations John Cox/Wildlife Art Agency

TEAMWORK

Dholes work together to bring down a chital, or axis deer (right). *Depending on the region, they will also join forces to hunt reindeer, wild boar, sambar deer, and wild sheep.*

UNFUSSY FEEDER

A raccoon dog snaps up a frog (left). *Small but resourceful, this canid has an almost boundless diet.*

Dholes have two basic hunting strategies. Led by a dominant male, the pack may spread out in line abreast and work their way through the scrub and long grass to flush out anything in their path. Small prey are quickly dispatched and snapped up by the nearest in line, but bigger quarry attracts the whole group for a concerted attack. The other tactic is more subtle, involving a division of forces in which half the pack enters thick forest vegetation and flushes the prey toward the others. In either case the dense cover may make coordination difficult, and the dholes keep track of each other by sound signals, including a curious short, fluting whistle.

The kill itself is messy but quick: The whole pack piles onto the victim and rips into it, tearing out its stomach so it dies of massive blood loss and shock within a few seconds. Then they start eating, fast. There is no squabbling over the spoils; dholes compete for food by simply bolting it down as quickly as they can, although an individual in possession of a particularly choice cut may carry it clear of its jostling pack mates. This type of prey sharing is characteristic of true pack hunters. Afterward they drink, lapping thirstily at the water or wallowing to cool down, before retiring to a favorite resting site to sleep off their meal. ■

589

SOCIAL STRUCTURE

Dogs tend to associate in groups; solitary or pair-living species are the exception rather than the norm, at least among the wolflike or lupine branch of the family. Even foxes may live in groups in the right circumstances, although they always forage alone. This suggests that the motive for group living is not pack hunting, as is often assumed, but some less easily defined social advantage. Hunting with the pack came later, as group-living dogs exploited their rapport to cooperatively trap and overwhelm ever bigger, more powerful prey.

The basis of dog society is the family unit: a mature male and female and their pups. In less gregarious species like the raccoon dog this seems to be the limit of sociability. The breeding pair form a close bond, but their pups apparently disperse at the end of summer and the family breaks up. The same pattern may occur among dingoes, but more typically some of the yearling pups stay within their parents' territory, living with them as a family group for another season or two. During this time their mother may whelp (give birth) again, and the young adults apparently help their parents rear the new pups by bringing food, standing guard, and even teaching the pups a few hunting tricks.

Dholes are always strongly social. As with dingoes the basic social unit is the family, consisting of a pair and their older offspring plus, in season, the breeding female's pups. Since a litter may number up to ten pups, such a family could well consist of ten or more adult dholes—enough for a formidable hunting pack. If the young adults stay within the family for more than a season, the pack may swell to 15 or 20, but larger groups are usually temporary liaisons between packs. Such "clans" may involve 40 animals or more, but they always split up into their component packs at the start of the mating period.

Within each pack there is a strict hierarchy. At the top are the alpha pair: the mated male and female, who are usually—but not invariably—the parents of the others. They dominate the other pack members, to the point of preventing them breeding even though they are sexually mature. In most packs there are twice as many males as females, suggesting that young females are evicted by the alpha female to prevent their breeding within their natal pack and diverting attention from her pups. A litter of eight or more pups takes a lot of feeding, and their mother relies on the assistance of the other members of the pack in this department.

For their part, the subordinate adults are willing to act as "helpers" because the pups are their close relatives and share some of their genes. Protecting and caring for them helps ensure the survival of a helper's genetic line so in effect the helpers are breeding by proxy within the security of the natal pack. At times, depending upon resources and nearby dhole density, this is a less risky option than dispersing to form packs of their own: Dispersal is the most dangerous phase of any adult dog's life, since it involves traveling through strange terrain and frequently running into trouble in the form of hunters, traps, roads, and rival adults of the same species.

Rod Williams/Bruce Coleman Ltd.

Within a dhole pack, most of the adults are closely related (above).

MOTHER'S HELP

The alpha (dominant) pair of any dingo pack can usually rely on the support of last year's litter when it comes to rearing the new pups (below).

The subordinate adults have a hierarchy of their own below the alpha pair. The pecking order is established by dominance struggles while the animals are still in the nursery, and maintained by ritual assertions of superiority or submission involving a subtle code of facial expression and body language. The social order is reestablished every morning when the rest of the pack come to the dominant male with their tails held low in submission, fawn on him, and rub their bodies together in a bonding ceremony before the day's hunting. This serves to cement the relationships between the pack members, reinforce status, and put them all in the same mood—a vital preliminary to an operation that relies on close empathy and efficient communication between the hunters. Pack hunting may not be the only reason for the strong social instinct among wild dogs, but it certainly depends on it. ■

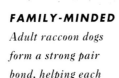

FAMILY-MINDED

Adult raccoon dogs form a strong pair bond, helping each other to rear young (above) *and often staying together for many years.*

(in) S I G H T

TERRITORIES

An average dhole pack hunts regularly within a home range of about 15 sq mi (40 sq km). The range is larger, however, in areas where both food and water are scarce. Dholes may defend the range as an exclusive pack territory, but the evidence for this is conflicting. There is little scent marking of boundaries, yet the way all the pack members use communal latrines sited at trail crossings and other key points suggests a deliberate territorial statement. In general, dholes seem to have a casual attitude to their neighbors and may even join forces with them to form large clans, although these clans break up in the breeding season.

Illustrations Chris Shields/Wildlife Art Agency

LIFE CYCLE

Male canids are unusually attentive fathers. For many mammals the paternal role begins and ends with courtship and mating, and the male maximizes his dynastic chances by impregnating as many females as possible. Among typical dogs and foxes, however, the male tries to make the most of each mating by working to ensure the survival of the pups that result. This involves a lot of time and energy, so he cannot generate too many families or he would be worn out. Accordingly, he tends to form a semipermanent pair bond with his mate. From a human point of view this may seem virtuous, but it is only a strategy. For a canid, male or female, looking after the family is just a way of securing the dynasty.

The raccoon dog is as conscientious as any. In northern Japan raccoon dogs mate in March or April, when they emerge from their winter hibernation, and immediately settle down to living as a pair. The four to eight young are born in a nursery burrow after a gestation of about two months, and the male brings food for their mother while she suckles them. As soon as the pups begin to take solid food, after a month or so, he brings food for them too. Eventually both parents share the job, foraging separately and carrying food back to the den. By the end of summer the pups are sufficiently well developed to forage for themselves and the family breaks up, although the pair bond may persist for several years.

In the dhole the pattern is more complex. Mating takes place within the social context of the pack, and if either of the previous season's dominant pair shows signs of weakness, there may be a revolution,

Like any other pups, young raccoon dogs engage in lively rough-and-tumble games.

PUP FIGHTS
are a mixture of play and real aggression (below); these lessons teach youngsters how to stand their ground against rivals, and also how to hunt.

PATERNAL RIGHTS
The male often becomes lodged inside his mate for a long period after mating (above). This actually benefits him, as it prevents other males from intruding and making their own bid for paternity.

WET NURSES
Occasionally two or more female dholes may appear to breed in the same den, but this is unlikely: Among social canids such tolerance is very rare. One explanation for den-sharing may be "phantom pregnancies" caused by hormonal imbalance. Although only one female in the pack actually gives birth, two or three may produce milk, and even suckle the pups of the alpha female.

GROWING UP

The life of a young dhole

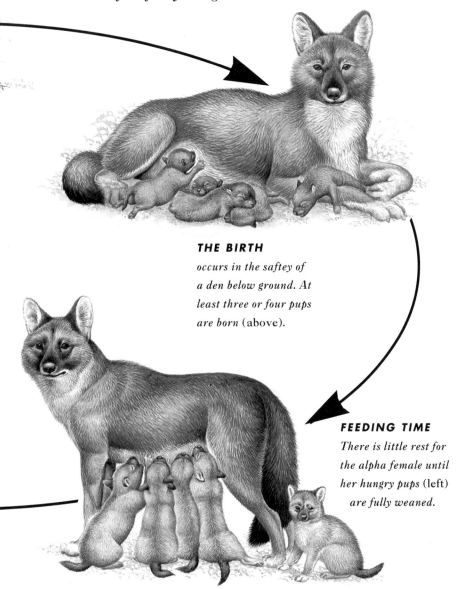

THE BIRTH

occurs in the saftey of a den below ground. At least three or four pups are born (above).

FEEDING TIME

There is little rest for the alpha female until her hungry pups (left) *are fully weaned.*

resulting in a subordinate or two moving up into "alpha" position. These new top dogs will then assert their dominance over the others, although defeated animals often leave to found new packs elsewhere.

Once the hierarchy has been resolved, the alpha pair mate. The whole pack moves into a suitable nursery den, which may be an abandoned porcupine burrow or similar hole, well disguised among dense vegetation, and after a two-month gestation five to ten pups are born. The mother relies on the alpha male and the rest of the pack to bring her food while she suckles the pups, and they do so by swallowing meat at the site of the kill and carrying it back to the den in their stomachs, regurgitating it on demand. Eventually they provide the same service for the pups until they are old enough, at about seven months, to begin hunting with the pack.

Meanwhile the family may have moved the den two or three times, either because they feel threatened or because the original den has become riddled with parasites. Normally several dholes guard the den site when the others are hunting, but they cannot defend against fleas. On their part the pups engage in their own battles for status, squabbling violently to establish a hierarchy of their own. They also play more peaceably, both among themselves and with the adults, chasing and ambushing one another in clear rehearsal for the more serious chases they will undertake when they become fully fledged hunters.

In the more remote parts of Australia dingoes may get a similar start in life, but usually the breeding pattern seems to be more like that of the raccoon dog, with young dingoes leaving their parents within the year to seek territories of their own. A breeding pair is less conspicuous than a pack, and the dingo, having been persecuted for two centuries, appears to have learned this lesson the hard way. ■

The female dingo suckles her litter on her feet, in the manner of a wolf.

Robin Budden/Wildlife Art Agency

FROM BIRTH TO DEATH

DHOLE	DINGO
GESTATION: 63 DAYS	**GESTATION:** 63 DAYS
LITTER SIZE: 4–10, AVERAGE 6	**LITTER SIZE:** 3–10, AVERAGE 5
BREEDING: MATE IN AUTUMN TO WINTER, GIVE BIRTH LATE WINTER TO EARLY SPRING	**BREEDING:** MATE IN AUTUMN, GIVE BIRTH LATE WINTER
EYES OPEN: 14 DAYS	**EYES OPEN:** 8–9 DAYS
FIRST LEAVE DEN: 3 MONTHS	**WEANING:** 2 MONTHS
HUNT WITH PACK: 7 MONTHS	**FIRST LEAVE DEN:** 3 MONTHS
SEXUAL MATURITY: 1 YEAR	**INDEPENDENCE:** 1 YEAR
LONGEVITY: 10 YEARS OR MORE IN THE WILD	**SEXUAL MATURITY:** 1 YEAR
	LONGEVITY: 10 YEARS OR MORE IN THE WILD

Gerard Lacz/NHPA

PERISHING IN OBSCURITY

DESPITE THEIR CLOSE AFFINITY WITH THE MOST CHERISHED OF HUMANKIND'S PETS, WILD DOGS ARE GENERALLY DESPISED AS CRUEL, WANTON KILLERS, AND THEY COULD EASILY SLIP UNMOURNED INTO EXTINCTION

H umans have a strange relationship with dogs. The domestic dog is humankind's best friend, pampered and petted throughout the world for thousands of years. The earliest remains of domestic dogs date from some 12,000 years ago at the end of the last Ice Age—at least 2,000 years before neolithic humans conceived the idea of domesticating sheep and goats as a source of meat on the hoof. These early domestic dogs can be identified because, although their bones resemble those of wolves, there are distinct differences. This means that the domestication process was well advanced and must have started long, long before. We can only speculate about how it started, but it is likely that orphaned wolf cubs were adopted as pets and possibly used for hunting. Either way, human and dog eventually developed a depth of understanding and affection that is probably unique between two such different species. The dingo appears to be a direct descendant of an early type of domestic dog, yet it inspires little understanding and affection. In fact, it is probably one of the most misunderstood, hated creatures on the Australian continent.

Paradoxically, raccoon dogs in the cold Siberian north grow poorer coats (below). *Those in central Russia, however, are valued for their pelts.*

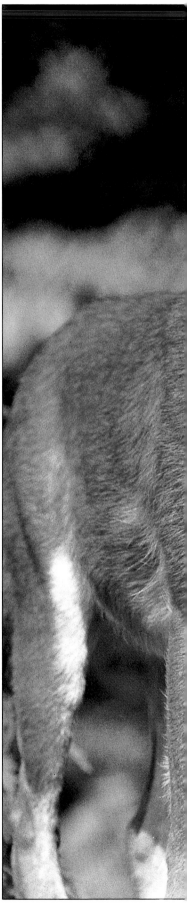

The dingo was first known to Europeans as early as 1623, when Dutch navigators found dingo tracks on the northern Queensland coast. Sightings by English seafarers in the late 17th century referred to "beasts like hungry wolves, lean like so many skeletons" and "as big as a mastiff dog." Tame dingoes were seen a century later by Captain James Cook, who witnessed pups being suckled by aboriginal women. But it was not until European settlers started to import their precious livestock to the Australian farms that the dingo fell from grace. By the turn of the 19th century, its persecution at the hands of humans had begun in earnest.

Widely regarded as a marauding sheep killer, it has been credited with all manner of atrocities including, notoriously, the abduction and devouring of a human baby. The notion that it might actually be relatively harmless, interesting, and worth encouraging is treated with derision by most of its human neighbors, despite the fact that many cherish pet dogs of their own.

DHOLES: DYING TO BE KNOWN

Meanwhile in southern Asia the dhole has acquired a nightmare notoriety as a hunter that slaughters its victims by ripping out their entrails—a bloody method of execution that, in the eyes of most people, makes the dhole a vile murderer quite unfit to be compared with magnificent predators like the tiger, the cheetah, and the lion. In truth the dhole's killing method is efficient, quick, and relatively painless,

---

DINGOES ARE STILL A PEST IN CERTAIN AGRICULTURAL AREAS, WHERE THEY ARE POISONED, SHOT, AND TRAPPED

---

since the victim usually dies of shock within seconds of being disemboweled. By contrast, an animal attacked by a tiger may take several minutes to die, fighting for breath as its windpipe is slowly crushed by the tiger's jaws, but since there is little blood, the tiger's tactic seems less barbarous.

These anticanine attitudes are important, for although both the dingo and the dhole are under threat, few people care. Indeed, the dhole has attracted so little interest that most people have never heard of it. One reason for this is its elusiveness—in fact, it was initially regarded as a myth by the British colonial authorities in India, who had no evidence for its existence beyond the lurid accounts provided by the locals. Today it is still a mysterious

Like the dingo, the dhole is a victim of lurid sensationalism and persecution in its homeland.

animal: Almost nothing is known of its habits outside India, and even within India it has been the subject of relatively few serious studies because it is so difficult to observe in the wild. In one study in the 1980s, some 5,000 hours of fieldwork resulted in roughly 100 hours of observation time—equivalent to one week per year. The lack of hard information means that many aspects of the dhole's ecology (its interaction with its environment) cannot be clarified, and this makes it very difficult to formulate an action plan for its conservation.

One thing is clear, though. The main reason for the dhole's decline—apart from direct persecution—is habitat loss. The rising human population has caused the destruction of vast areas of forest, scrub, and steppe through agricultural expansion and overgrazing by domestic animals. This has both reduced the living area available to the dhole and eliminated many of the animals it preys upon. A small, unspecialized omnivore like the raccoon dog

SCIENTISTS STILL HAVE MUCH TO LEARN ABOUT THE DHOLE BEFORE THEY CAN SET UP EFFECTIVE CONSERVATION MEASURES

may be able to weather such transformations by modifying its diet and retreating to small pockets of surviving wilderness, but a high-profile predator like the dhole needs space. These days space is a scarce commodity in southern Asia, and, as a result, many of the surviving dhole populations are fragmented and scattered. Inevitably several of these will dwindle and vanish, either through disease—wild canids are prone to a wide variety of diseases including rabies, distemper, and anthrax—or through inbreeding. Normally there is a regular exchange of genetic material between populations as young animals disperse across country, but if a population is confined to a particular tract of country by encircling development, such dispersal is impossible. As a result, the animals find mates closer to home and there is no infusion of fresh blood. Each succeeding generation becomes progressively more inbred, with potentially disastrous results.

FERAL HYBRIDS

The opposite problem threatens the dingo. Despite having been shot, trapped, and poisoned relentlessly for 200 years, it remains fairly numerous, although over most of its range it is almost as elusive as the dhole and equally mysterious. The big dingo packs of folklore seem to have vanished, probably through persecution pressure, but although it mostly lives in pairs and small groups, the dingo has plenty of scope for outbreeding. Too much, in fact.

W. Weisser/Ardea

ENDANGERED SPECIES

THE STATELESS DINGO

Many wild animals are reckoned to be pests of some sort, but few have been so wholly hated as the dingo. Not only is it persecuted throughout most of Australia, but it has also been denied official status as a native wild animal—a status that would give it some sort of right to survive.

The justification for this is the dingo's shady history as an introduced mammal. Australia has no truly native dogs, since the canids belong to the group of mammals known as the placentals—after the placenta that nourishes them in the womb. These failed to reach Australia before it became isolated from the other continents some 40 million years ago and drifted off into the Indo-Pacific Ocean with its living freight of marsupials (pouched mammals).

Nearly all the placental mammals currently found in Australia—cats and rats, sheep and goats, rabbits and stoats—have been introduced either deliberately or accidentally by humans since the European settlement, and most of them have created serious problems for the native marsupials by either killing them or competing with them for food. Marsupials in general seem poorly equipped to cope with this and have suffered accordingly; in consequence, all introduced animals—those that have gone wild, at least—are regarded as pests, to be destroyed at every opportunity.

So far, so good. Cats, rats, and rabbits are recent introductions to Australia and threaten the future of a unique endemic

CONSERVATION MEASURES

• The International Union for the Conservation of Nature (IUCN) has commissioned an action plan for conserving wild dogs. The idea of the plan is to determine which species need conserving, and how best to do it with the resources available. Although the zoologists involved are hampered by lack of information, their recommendations carry the backing of the IUCN and will have to be taken seriously by national governments.

fauna. They are also widely distributed throughout the world, so if they vanished from Australia, their survival as species would not be jeopardized. But the principle has also been extended to the dingo, an animal that colonized Australia at least 3,500 years ago. Since that time it has developed into a distinct subspecies that exists nowhere else, and if it could be proved that it reached Australia unaided by humans—by swimming across the Torres Strait from New Guinea, say—then it might qualify as a native, just like the bats that made the same journey by air. Sadly for the dingo it was probably introduced as a pet. As a pet, all was well. As a competitor with humans, the friendship is broken and not easily mended.

WILD DOGS IN DANGER

THE CHART BELOW SHOWS HOW THE INTERNATIONAL UNION FOR THE CONSERVATION OF NATURE (IUCN) CLASSIFIES THE STATUS OF THE WILD DOGS OF SOUTHERN ASIA AND AUSTRALIA:

DHOLE	VULNERABLE

VULNERABLE MEANS THAT THE SPECIES IS LIKELY TO DECLINE AND BECOME CLASSIFIED AS *ENDANGERED* IF NOTHING IS DONE TO IMPROVE ITS SITUATION.

Ford Kristo/Planet Earth Pictures

THE UNLOVED AND EXILED DINGO IS SURVIVING IN THE REMOTE OUTBACK—BUT FOR HOW LONG?

• There is now a move—albeit rather a belated one—to have the dingo recognized as a native Australian mammal. However, this is opposed by farming lobbies, who fear that if the dingo is not controlled, it will breed rapidly and threaten their livelihoods. A compromise arrangement involving limited protection and licensed, seasonal control may be eventually endorsed as the solution.

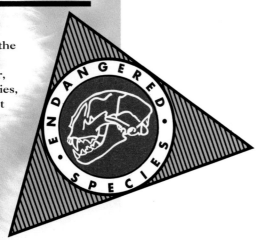

One reason the dingo is classified as a type of domestic dog is its readiness to mate with other domestic dogs and produce fertile hybrids. Their mutual ancestor, the wolf, is capable of such inter-breeding but normally avoids it; the dingo seems to court it, and, as a result, many wild "dingoes" are actually dingo/dog crosses. These hybrids are hard to identify, for they generally inherit the dingo build and, although their coloration varies from pale brindle to gray or black, the coat colors of purebred dingoes also vary from the characteristic ginger-yellow to black-and-tan and even white.

This confusion has encouraged the idea that all dingoes are just tame dogs gone wild, and therefore pests, but there are differences. A true dingo has a more massive head than a domestic dog, with bigger, longer teeth. It also has much larger eardrums. More significant, a female comes in heat only once a year, like a wolf, whereas most domestic bitches come in heat twice a year—indicating that it is a distinct race and not just a wild form of mongrel. Unfortunately, if hybridization continues at the present rate, this distinct race could disappear, swamped by the tide of domestic genes, and the dingo—the true, wild dingo that colonized Australia thousands of years before the arrival of the European settlers—could become effectively extinct.

THRIVING IN OBSCURITY

While the big canids dwindle through habitat loss, persecution, disease, and genetic pollution, the small, adaptable raccoon dog seems to flourish, particularly in eastern Europe. Its first big break came in 1928 or 1929, when over 400 pregnant females were introduced into European Russia to boost the trade in pelts. Although this introduction was not overly successful, subsequent attempts in 1934–35 and 1936 enabled the raccoon dog to colonize many regions of the former Soviet Union. In Kalinin Province near Volgograd, for example, they bred so successfully

ALONGSIDE MAN

DOMESTICATION

The dingo probably came to Australia 4,000–6,000 years ago, in the boats of traders from Southeast Asia. The traders came to barter goods with the native Australian people, whose ancestors had colonized the continent some 30,000 years before, and the dogs may have been pets or even a live food source—dog meat is esteemed a delicacy in many parts of Southeast Asia.

The aboriginal Australians may have trained dingoes for hunting, but there is no hunting-dog tradition in aboriginal culture and modern dingoes have proved very difficult to train. It is more likely that they treated them as pets in a loose fashion, allowing them to scavenge around the camp and occasionally petting them or sleeping with them for warmth in the subfreezing temperatures of the desert night. Pariahs—half-wild domestic mongrels—are treated in much the same way today, as are dingoes in remoter parts of the continent.

Despite this loose association with humans, the dingo essentially went wild when it reached Australia, finding its own food supply and breeding in total isolation without any artificial control or selection. This means that it is a living relic of an early stage in the process that turned the wolf into the domestic dog, having missed out on the last few thousand years of selective breeding. Nevertheless, the dingo is a product of humankind and is now neither wolf nor dog. Whether and how to preserve its unique character is likely to continue to be a difficult puzzle.

that, by 1946, the annual harvest of raccoon dog pelts was more than twice that of any region in the Far East.

The species is now firmly established over a wide range in European Russia, from the Volga River to the Caucasus and the Black Sea. It is widespread also in the Ukraine, in the Astrakhan region, and in Belorussia. Its numbers have fallen in eastern Siberia and other parts of its native range, mainly through hunting and habitat disturbance; in Japan it has suffered from a brisk trade in its flesh and in its fur: Each year roughly 70,000 raccoon dogs are killed for their pelts in Japan.

Between 1929 and 1967 about 8,650 raccoon dogs were released into Russia for the fur industry. The trade continues today, although to a reduced degree.

Elsewhere there is now little demand for its fur, and in Europe it has become rather a nuisance. It reached Finland in 1935, entering Sweden in 1945, Romania in 1951, and Poland in 1955. Over the ensuing decades the raccoon dog steadily invaded Europe, expanding its range by an average of 85 mi (135 km) each year. The species has fully invaded Germany and is now marching through Switzerland and the Netherlands. It has been implicated in the transmission of rabies, partly because it carries the disease and partly because its westward spread since the 1930s has roughly mirrored that of the current rabies epidemic. However, rabies may yet be eliminated in Europe by an immunization program using bait laced with an oral vaccine, and since this will benefit raccoon dogs as well as the native wildlife, it is probably in Europe to stay. ∎

Darek Karp/NHPA

INTO THE FUTURE

Out in the baked red heart of Australia, away from the insidious threat of hybridization with feral pariah dogs, the immediate future of the dingo is probably secure—provided the rabbit supply holds up. By degrees, dingoes are becoming specialists at hunting rabbits, and since rabbits are a serious problem throughout Australia, there may come a day when sheep farmers will begin to value the dingo as a pest-control agent.

While the dingo depends on rabbits, the dhole may depend on the tiger—but for very different reasons. Wild dogs will probably never capture the public imagination as a conservation cause, but luckily for the dhole, it shares part of its range with the most charismatic of all endangered species. The tiger crisis has become a matter of worldwide concern, and since the only way of conserving the tiger

PREDICTION

CONTINUING SUCCESS

Adaptable and secretive, the raccoon dog will probably continue its spread across Europe and become more common in the West than it is in its native range.

effectively has to be the preservation of large areas of its natural habitat, ecologically intact, the dhole can only benefit—along with a whole host of obscure Asian animals whose future has been put in jeopardy by human population growth.

The great problem with this, of course, is the precarious position of the lead player in the drama. The tiger has already vanished from much of its former range and, sadly, looks set to disappear from most of the rest, mainly through poor preserve management and poaching, which continues in defiance of international law. If the tiger fades from the scene, the main incentive for conserving its habitat will fade with it, and while the public turns its attention elsewhere, the dhole could slip quietly into oblivion. ■

ROYAL SANCTUARIES

It is no accident that India remains the prime stronghold of the dhole, for there is a long tradition of wildlife conservation throughout the Indian subcontinent. The concept is enshrined in Hindu scripture, and as early as the 4th century B.C. the *Arthasastra*, a manual of statecraft, advocated setting aside forest preserves for wild animals. More recently great tracts of wild country were preserved as hunting ranges by Indian princes, including Ranthambhore in India and Royal Chitwan in Nepal. Ranthambhore was once the hunting ground of the maharajah of Jaipur, and the spectacular remains of the maharajah's forts, temples, and hunting lodges still survive amid the forests that are now one of the main refuges for the dhole and the tiger. Ranthambhore is also the focus of new conservation initiatives spearheaded by an organization called the Ranthambhore Foundation, which aims to square the needs of local communities with the urgent need to protect the remaining virgin forest and the animals that live within it.

DINGO DILEMMA

Rabbits destroy pasture by nibbling it to the ground, making it useless to sheep, and when the Australian rabbit population was virtually annihilated by disease in the 1950s, farm profits increased by the equivalent of $76 million in the first year—at 1950s prices. If the dingo population was destroyed overnight in a similar fashion, the sheep farmers would probably rejoice, but any gains made through the disappearance of potential sheep killers would probably be canceled severalfold by the ensuing plague of rabbits.

Illustration Carol Roberts

INDEX

Published by Marshall Cavendish Corporation
99 White Plains Road
Tarrytown, New York 10591-9001

© Marshall Cavendish Corporation, 1997

Library of Congress Cataloging-in-Publication Data

Encyclopedia of mammals.
    p. cm.
    Includes index.
    ISBN 0-7614-0575-5 (set)   ISBN 0-7614-0579-8 (v. 4)

    Summary: Detailed articles cover the history, anatomy, feeding habits, social structure, reproduction, territory,
        and current status of ninety-five mammals around the world.
    1. Mammals—Encyclopedias, Juvenile. [1. Mammals—Encyclopedias.] I. Marshall Cavendish Corporation.
    QL706.2.E54 1996
    599'.003—dc20   96-17736
                                                                                        CIP
                                                                                        AC

Printed in Malaysia
Bound in U.S.A.